FREEDOM, ENJOYMENT, AND HAPPINESS

FREEDOM, ENJOYMENT, AND HAPPINESS

An Essay on Moral Psychology

RICHARD WARNER

Cornell University Press
Ithaca and London

First published 1987 by Cornell University Press.

International Standard Book Number 0-8014-1977-8
Library of Congress Catalog Card Number 86-19696
Printed in the United States of America

Librarians: Library of Congress cataloging information
appears on the last page of the book.

To Johnna
Das Unzulängliche
Hier wird's Ereignis

Contents

Acknowledgments

Paul Grice has—in a variety of ways—influenced my thoughts about the topics in this book (I will not speculate on the extent to which he would agree with the result), and I am very much in his debt. I am also greatly indebted to Andreas Eshetê, with whom I discussed most of the ideas presented here and who was so often right. A particularly special acknowledgment goes to Johnna Hansen; she not only gave good advice on what to say and how to say it, she also provided support and encouragement as she lived (suffered) through the writing of it. Others who kept me from wrong paths are David Copp, John Dreher, Hartry Field, Gregg Galardi, Catharine Hantzis, Barbara Herman, Jonathan Jacobs, Janet Levin, Brian Loar, Edwin McCann, Thomas Ricketts, Stephen Schiffer, Christopher Stone, Joseph Volpe, Gary Watson, and Dallas Willard.

I owe thanks to Madelyne Drewe, Jo Kolsum, Sandra Natson, and Julia Spezia for typing, considerable patience, and numerous favors.

I also thank, for their coffee and hospitality, Kelly and Cohen's and Fiesta Pizza (both in Philadelphia) and The Jamaica Bay Inn Coffee Shop (in Marina del Rey).

A portion of the Introduction is a revised version of my article "Grice on Happiness," published in *Philosophical Grounds of Rationality*, a volume I coedited with Richard Grandy (Oxford University Press, 1986). Parts of Chapter 4 appeared, in somewhat

9

different form, in my "Enjoyment," *Philosophical Review*, 89 (October 1980), 507–526. I am grateful to the publishers for permission to use this reworked material.

RICHARD WARNER

Venice, California

FREEDOM, ENJOYMENT, AND HAPPINESS

> What is a man,
> If his chief good and market of his time
> Be but to sleep and feed? A beast, no more.
> Sure he that made us with such large discourse,
> Looking before and after, gave us not
> That capability and godlike reason
> To fust in us unused.
>
> —*Hamlet*

> ...to live is, in itself, a value judgment. To breathe is to judge.
>
> —ALBERT CAMUS, *The Rebel*

Introduction

What is it to lead a happy life? The question is of sufficient interest in its own right to merit a detailed philosophical discussion, and this is my main—but not my only—reason for devoting this book to answering that question. The account of happiness I will propose is based on an account of personhood, which is in turn based on an account of freedom. In this way, the analysis of happiness presents a systematic picture of the relations among happiness, freedom, and personhood.

These relations have typically being ignored by philosophers working in the British Empiricist tradition and by Anglo-American analytic philosophy generally.[1] One pervasive tendency has been to identify happiness with having a sufficient amount of enjoyment or pleasure. Sidgwick, for example, says that by the phrase "the greatest possible Happiness" he understands "the greatest attainable surplus of pleasure over pain; the two terms being used, with equally comprehensive meanings, to include respectively all kinds of agreeable and disagreeable feelings."[2] This entirely ignores con-

---

1. John Stuart Mill is a notable exception; see Richard Wollheim, "John Stuart Mill and Isaiah Berlin," in Alan Ryan, ed., *The Idea of Freedom* (Oxford: Oxford University Press, 1979). Dewey is another exception (as Chris Stone pointed out to me).

2. Henry Sidgwick, *The Methods of Ethics*, 7th ed. (Indianapolis/Cambridge, Mass.: Hackett, 1981), pp. 120–121.

nections among happiness, freedom, and personhood—connections that must be considered in any adequate treatment of happiness. The same criticism applies to two other accounts of happiness that enjoy some intuitive appeal. The first is that happiness consists in having enough of one's most important wants satisfied;[3] the second, that one is leading a happy life if and only if one is pleased with one's life as a whole.[4] Unless more is said (e.g., an explanation of the relevant sense of 'important'), both analyses ignore relations with freedom and personhood.

These relations—or relations very much like them—have been noted by philosophers outside Anglo-American analytic philosophy. Aristotle is one example; Hegel is another; as is Kierkegaard. Unfortunately, the discussions these philosophers offer of freedom, personhood, and happiness are—even in the case of Aristotle— notoriously problematic and opaque and involve assumptions that seem quite dubious (such as Aristotle's assumption that the universe has a teleological structure). My aim is to give a clear analysis of the relations that is free of dubious assumptions. The analysis makes the relations explicit—revealing the concept of leading a happy life as a crucial nexus at which the concepts of personhood and freedom join with other concepts such as enjoyment, desire, and the justification of action.

The concept of justification of action figures in the account of freedom and, via that account, in the accounts of personhood and happiness. Given the central role the notion of justification plays, it may seem that I should give some explanation of what it is for an action to be justified—where this explanation is given prior to, or at least independently of, the accounts of freedom, personhood, and happiness. However, it is not necessary to do this. The following gloss is sufficient for my purposes: a justification of an action is a consideration that—in a principled and nonarbitrary way— weighs, to some degree, in favor of performing the action. The rationale for the "to some degree" qualification is that to count as a justification for an action, a consideration need not be a decisive justification, a consideration that shows the action to be better jus-

3. Von Wright discusses this sort of account in *The Varieties of Goodness* (London: Routledge and Kegan Paul, 1963), pp. 92–94.

4. Elizabeth Telfer develops such an account in *Happiness* (New York: St. Martin's, 1980).

tified than any other alternative; the requirement is merely that the consideration weigh to some—perhaps minimal—degree in favor of performing the action.

It is worth illustrating the notion of justification with one example. You ask me why I am eating a piece of chocolate. I realize that you suspect that I am eating just to be polite and that you are asking for a consideration, other than politeness, that weights in favor of my eating the chocolate. I answer, "I want it," meaning that I want it just for the sake of the taste and not as a means to any end such as politeness. Here, I offer my desire as the requested justification, and although I argue in Chapter 1 that a desire is not always a justification for action, let us suppose that in this case my desire really does provide a justification. Indeed, suppose—to take an extreme but clear case—that satisfying the desire is entirely harmless; satisfying the desire has no negative or adverse consequences whatsoever. Then surely the desire is a consideration that weighs in favor of my eating the chocolate. (This is intended as an especially clear case; I am not suggesting that a desire provides a justification only when satisfying the desire has no negative consequences.)

I could, instead of talking of justification, talk of a reason for action—understanding a reason for action to be a consideration that weighs in favor of performing the action. But 'reason for action' has other meanings, so it is clearer to talk of justification (not that 'justification' is all that unambiguous, but it seems easier to keep the relevant sense in mind).[5]

I have another reason, apart from the fact that it is unnecessary, for not giving an analysis of justification independently of the accounts of freedom, personhood, and happiness. I want—ultimately—to use the role of the notion of justification in those accounts as a guide to what the exact content of the notion is: seeing how justification functions is the key to seeing its content. This is why the book bears the subtitle "An Essay on Moral Psychology," for while the scope of the question "What is it for an action to be justified?" extends beyond moral philosophy, the question is certainly a central concern in a philosophical treatment of morality.

5. For some relevant senses of 'reason', see Bernard Williams, "External and Internal Reasons," in *Moral Luck* (Cambridge: Cambridge University Press, 1981).

This approach to justification is motivated in part by a view (which I will state but not defend) about the current state of moral philosophy. I think there is (still) a good deal of truth in G. E. M. Anscombe's remark in "Modern Moral Philosophy" (1957) that "it is not profitable for us at present to do moral philosophy; that should be laid aside at any rate until we have an adequate philosophy of psychology, in which we are conspicuously lacking.[6] At a minimum, "an adequate philosophy of psychology" should provide moral philosophy with an informative picture of what it is for an action to be justified. This book is intended as a contribution to developing such a picture. It carries out the first half of the proposed explication of the concept of justification: showing that the notion of justification does indeed play a certain systematic role in the accounts of freedom, personhood, and happiness.

By 'account' I mean a set of necessary and sufficient conditions— a "conceptual analysis"; for the sake of stylistic variation, I will use 'analysis' and 'definition' as synonyms for 'account'. Those who reject any nontrivial analytic/synthetic distinction may find it at best old-fashioned, and at worst wrong, to offer such conceptual analyses. I will not address this issue except to say, first, that my aim is to give illuminating and informative accounts of various concepts and, second, that the concepts in question are amenable to analysis—the proof is in the doing. And it can be done; analyses that are remarkably counterexample-proof can be given. I think giving such analyses is consistent with the rejection of any non-trivial analytic/synthetic distinction (we simply have to explain their invulnerability to counterexamples in some other way). In any case, the undertaking is essential. We simply do not at present have any adequate, systematic picture of the relations among happiness,

---

6. G. E. M. Anscombe, "Modern Moral Philosophy," *Philosophy*, 33 (1957), 1–19. She continues: "In present-day philosophy an explanation is required of how an unjust man is a bad man, or an unjust action a bad one; to give such an explanation belongs to ethics; but it cannot even be begun until we are equipped with a sound philosophy of psychology. For the proof that an unjust man is a bad man would require a positive account of what *type of characteristic* a virtue is—a problem not of ethics, but of conceptual analysis—and how it relates to the action instanced, a matter which I think Aristotle did not succeed in really making clear." Anscombe's focus on virtue is not incompatible with my focus on justification. Anscombe has Aristotle in mind, and virtuous action is, for Aristotle, action for which there is a certain sort of justification.

freedom, personhood, and justification; without such a picture, we are doing moral philosophy largely in the dark, without an adequate understanding of the key concepts.

Now let us turn to a terminological point. In the foregoing discussion, I used 'happiness' and 'leading a happy life' interchangeably. Unfortunately, neither expression unambiguously captures the concept I have in mind, so I will devote the rest of this Introduction to characterizing that concept. The first step is to distinguish between feeling happy and leading a happy life. To feel happy one must have a certain sort of *experience*, and one can have an experience of the appropriate sort yet not be leading a happy life: one morning I find myself in a euphoric mood, but when you remark that you have not seen me so happy in a long time, I paint a bleak picture of my circumstances and prospects. My euphoria is just a brief bit of cheerfulness in my otherwise unrelieved misery at my failures. I feel happy, but I am not leading a happy life. Conversely, one can be leading a happy life at a given time without feeling happy at that time. You might correctly regard yourself as leading a happy life even though you are momentarily depressed; you see your depression as a mere transient mood occurring against the background of a way of life that as a rule you find fully satisfying.

It is leading a happy life that is my concern here, but (except when I am talking about *feeling* happy) I will continue to use 'happy' and 'leading a happy life' interchangeably. I will understand both expressions as true of a person throughout longer or shorter periods of time. Thus Jones may not have led a happy life the first two years he was in New York, may have lived a happy life for the next four years, and then may have ceased to live a happy life for the next two years. This does not mean that we cannot ask whether Jones is leading a happy life when the relevant period includes all eight years in New York—when, for example, the period is his entire life; the answer might be yes, even though the eight years in New York include four unhappy years. The happy periods may compensate sufficiently for the unhappy ones.

Talking in this way about leading a happy life may seem problematic. It would seem that we cannot coherently describe someone as leading a happy *life* during a certain period of time if that period is too short. Indeed, something stronger is true. Imagine just arbitrarily selecting some continuous segment of a person's life—say, from June 30, 1980, to April 20, 1983. Suppose this segment does not coincide with any natural demarcation of periods in the person's life, a demarcation one would make for descriptive or explanatory purposes. It may be quite inappropriate to raise the question of whether a person is leading a happy life during such an arbitrarily selected segment. So how do we demarcate the periods for which it is appropriate to raise the question? I answer this question in Chapter 5; until then I will frequently suppress reference to the relevant period of time when describing someone as leading a happy life.

Perhaps it would be better to avoid the expression 'leading a happy life'; some use, for what I am calling leading a happy life, expressions like 'well being', 'living well', or—what some may regard as best—'being self-fulfilled'. Perhaps it would be even better to use a neologism like 'getting along self-fulfillingly'. But I will use none of these expressions. We do sometimes use 'leading a happy life' for the concept I have in mind, and in any case, the form of expression does not really matter, for I will give an explicit characterization of the concept.[7] This characterization identifies four features; failure to exhibit any one of them is—it would seem— enough to make one count as not leading a happy life; possession of all four features is—it would seem—sufficient for leading a happy life.

The reason for the "it would seem" qualification is that this initial characterization of leading a happy life is merely preliminary and is intended only as a *condition of adequacy* on any subsequent definition of leading a happy life. Any definition should entail each of the four conditions of the initial characterization or, failing that, should provide a basis for explaining why any condition not entailed is not really a condition of leading a happy life. In addition, the initial characterization leaves a number of crucial questions unanswered. Any adequate account should answer (or at least provide a basis for answering) these questions. In Chapter 5, I will give a second account of happiness, which meets this condition of ad-

---

7. See Richard Kraut's interesting discussion in "Two Conceptions of Happiness," *Philosophical Review*, 88 (April 1979). Kraut's discussion provides some reasons for sticking with 'happiness'.

equacy. But now let us examine the first condition of the initial account.

> 1. One is leading a happy life only if one satisfies (is in the process of satisfying) one's important desires sufficiently often.

We act so as to satisfy a variety of desires, and one reason we act on the desires that we do is that we think that in satisfying them we will be leading happy lives. If one is leading a life severely deficient in the satisfaction of desires, one is not leading a happy life.

To see what it means to say that one must satisfy one's *important* desires, suppose Jane wants to attain and use political power, to travel, to see her friends, and to read extensively. Now, it could be a fact about Jane that her happiness depends on satisfying these desires: failure to do so will result in her not leading a happy life. It is this fact that I am expressing by calling the desires 'important'. Of course, a noncircular account of happiness cannot explain the notion of importance in this way; I will provide a noncircular explanation in Chapter 5. At that time, I will also provide support for an assumption that I have tacitly made here: that each person has desires that are important in the relevant sense. This assumption is not implausible. *Typically*, there is, for each person, a range of desires such that the person's happiness depends on satisfying those desires. What needs argument is that this *must* be true for each person.

But why require that one satisfy one's important desires sufficiently often? Because one way to be unhappy is to fail to satisfy one's important desires *often enough*. Suppose Jane succeeds in attaining the political power that has been her single-minded aim. Yet she is unhappy, for she still desires to see her friends, to travel, and to read extensively. She virtually had to give up satisfying these other desires to attain and use political power, and this sacrifice has resulted in her not leading a happy life: she is not satisfying her important desires sufficiently often.

To illustrate the interaction between the "importance" requirement and the "sufficiently often" requirement, note that Jane's single-minded pursuit of political power could have made her happy if the desire for it had been important enough. Imagine Jane in the midst of her success. She realizes she has given up much. But it does not matter, for in attaining and using political power, she is leading a happy life since the importance of the desire satisfied compensates for the desires whose satisfaction she forgoes.

We are left with three unanswered questions. How do we give a noncircular explanation of the notion of an important desire? Why should we think that each person has desires that are important in this sense? And—a question suppressed during the discussion of the "sufficiently often" requirement—what counts as satisfying one's important desires sufficiently often? These questions must remain unanswered until our discussion of the second account of happiness, and this is true of another question as well: is it really true, as the first condition asserts, that one must actually satisfy one's desires to lead a happy life—as opposed merely to *thinking* one is doing so? Consider the following example.

A restaurant owner prides himself on his astute business sense that—in his eyes—has guided the restaurant through difficult times and has built it into a success. He also takes great pleasure in the love and respect of his wife and children. In reality, the owner has no business sense whatsoever. The manager really runs the restaurant, but to preserve his job he adroitly conceals this fact from the owner. But all of the employees, as well as the owner's wife and children, know the true situation. The children regard their father as a buffoon and join with the employees in laughing at him behind his back. His wife is having an affair with the manager.

According to the first requirement, the owner is not leading a happy life. But is this correct? After all, he thinks he is getting what he wants.

> 2. One is leading a happy life only if one believes that one
> is satisfying one's important desires sufficiently often.[8]

Far from being a clear fact about happiness, this requirement may seem quite dubious. Couldn't a person satisfy his important desires

---

8. There is an ambiguity here. Does the person believe, *of a certain set of desires,* that he is satisfying those desires sufficiently often? Or does he believe that *there is some set or other* such that he is satisfying those desires sufficiently often? It is the former reading that is correct, as we will see in Chapter 5.

sufficiently often, yet be so unreflective that he never formed the belief that he was doing so? If so, why should his being so unreflective exclude him from happiness? Nonetheless, philosophical accounts of happiness frequently require that the happy person have a belief about the extent to which he is successful in satisfying his desires. Rawls, for example, says that "a person is happy . . . during those periods when he is successfully carrying through a rational plan, *and he is with reason confident that his efforts will come to fruition.*"[9] Aristotle takes the belief that one is acting in accord with virtue to be an essential component of *eudaimonia*;[10] Hume makes it clear that, because of the way passion; and imagination interact, one's happiness depends crucially and unavoidably on one's estimate of the extent to which one's desires will be satisfied.[11]

It would be surprising, then, if we could not find considerations that adequately motivate the second requirement—and we can. Consider the role of "It makes him/her happy" in the explanation of action. Imagine that Jones spends long hours day after day practicing sailing. As you and I watch Jones execute one maneuver after another, I wonder what motivates him to expend such effort, what makes him get up every morning and begin to practice. You answer, "It makes him happy." Your answer does not merely point out that in sailing day after day Jones is satisfying his important desires sufficiently often; it also attributes to Jones a motive that (at least partially) explains why he gets up every morning and begins to practice. Let us call this motive the 'affirmative attitude'. It is part of our concept of happiness that the happy person has such an affirmative attitude. Recognizing this fact is the best way to account for the explanatory role of "It makes him/her happy."

9. John Rawls, *A Theory of Justice* (Cambridge: Harvard University Press, 1971), p. 512.

10. I discuss this aspect of Aristotle's views in "Grice on Happiness," in Richard Grandy and Richard Warner, eds., *Philosophical Grounds of Rationality: Intentions, Categories, Ends* (Oxford: Oxford University Press, 1986). The basic idea is that to fail to form beliefs about whether one's activity is in conformity with virtue would be to fail to exhibit practical wisdom (see *Nicomachean Ethics*, 1144a23–25), and to fail to exhibit practical wisdom is to fail to be in conformity with virtue (1144b31–1145a2) and hence to fail to be happy since happiness, for Aristotle, is (roughly) activity in conformity with virtue.

11. See David Hume, *A Treatise of Human Nature*, 2d ed., ed. L. A. Selby-Bigge (Oxford: Oxford University Press, 1978), Book II, Part III.

It is plausible to suggest that the happy person has the affirmative attitude because (in part, at least) he believes he is satisfying his important desires sufficiently often; he is aware of his own success. This is why the considerations about the affirmative attitude support the second requirement. The question here, of course, is: how are we to characterize the happy person's affirmative attitude?

> 3. One is leading a happy life only if, in addition to satisfying one's important desires sufficiently often, one enjoys satisfying those desires.

One certainly does not count as happy if one's life is utterly devoid of enjoyment or if enjoyments are too few and far between. One must enjoy the satisfaction of one's important desires. This is an additional requirement over and above the demand that one satisfy enough of one's desires, for enjoyment cannot be identified with the mere satisfaction of desire (as I argue in Chapter 4). One may desire to see *Star Wars*; one may even desire to see it for its own sake, yet fail to enjoy the movie.

Imagine this happening on a large scale. A businessman believes his happiness consists entirely in becoming and being president of the company. He satisfies this desire but finds his success empty. His problem is not that he wants something else. There is no way of life that he sees as better or more desirable; indeed, in satisfying his desire to be president, and the desires clustering around that central desire, he is satisfying his important desires sufficiently often. His problem, as he is dismayed to discover, is that he does not enjoy the satisfaction of these desires. His situation is exactly analogous to the *Star Wars* example except that the divorce between desire-satisfaction and enjoyment occurs throughout the most central aspect of his life. A person in such circumstances is not leading a happy life.

The third requirement does not, as stated, capture what is perhaps the most important aspect of the relation between happiness and enjoyment: the way in which both concepts are related to the concept of self. William James makes this point forcefully in *The Principles of Psychology*. " I am," James writes,

> often confronted by the necessity of standing by one of my empirical selves and relinquishing the rest. Not that I would not, if I could,

be both handsome and fat and well dressed, and a great athlete, and make a million a year, be a wit, a *bon vivant*, and a lady killer, as well as a philosopher, a philanthropist, statesman, warrior, and African explorer, as well as a 'tone poet' and saint. But the thing is simply impossible. The millionaire's work would run counter to the saint's; the *bon vivant* and the philanthropist would trip each other; the philosopher and the lady killer could not well keep house in the same tenement of clay. Such different characters may conceivably at the outset of life be alike *possible* to a man. But to make any one of them actual, the rest must more or less be suppressed. So the seeker of his truest, strongest, deepest self must review the list carefully, and pick out the one on which to stake his salvation. All other selves thereupon become unreal, but the fortunes of this self are real. Its failures are real failures, its triumphs real triumphs, carrying shame and gladness with them.[12]

While his language is perhaps more picturesque than perspicuous, James's "standing by one of my empirical selves" does clearly describe something related, as the passage suggests, to enjoyment ("shame and gladness") and happiness (since one picks a self "on which to stake his salvation"—reading 'salvation' as a hyperbolic reference to happiness). The question here is: what are the important relations among happiness, enjoyment, and the self?

> 4. One is leading a happy life only if, in addition to satisfying one's important desires sufficiently often, what one desires: (a) one takes to be worthy of desire and (b) really is worthy of desire.

What makes (a) plausible is that it would seem to be the antithesis of a happy life to spend a life in the pursuit of ends that one—the very person pursuing those ends—fails to regard as worthy of pursuit. This intuition can be explained by a further development of the idea that the happy person has an "affirmative attitude" toward his life. In discussing the second requirement, I said that the happy person has this attitude in part at least because he believes he is satisfying his important desires sufficiently often. What I want to suggest here is that this affirmative attitude may be the result not only of this belief but also of the belief that his ends are worthwhile.

12. William James, *The Principles of Psychology* (New York: Dover, 1980), I, pp. 309–310.

To fail to have the latter belief is to fail to have the affirmative attitude that is, in part, definitive of the happy person. Or so I suggest; I will argue for the suggestion in Chapter 5.

In Chapter 5, I will also argue *against* the (b) part of the fourth requirement. However, it is worth noting that the (b) requirement is not unmotivated. Suppose someone—The Counter—supports himself as a computer programmer. He regards this as a mere means to the pursuit of the activity to which he devotes all the time he possibly can: counting blades of grass. He lays out geometric patterns with string and counts the blades of grass within—recording location, date, pattern, and number. He regards this activity as worthy of desire.

One response is that The Counter is wrong: counting blades of grass is not worthy of desire and, *therefore*, The Counter is not leading a happy life (a life so misspent is not a happy one). I think this response is incorrect, but my aim here is simply to acknowledge the opposite intuition. (In the Afterword, I will suggest that the issues about worthiness come down to the question of the exact content of the notion of justification that figures in the accounts of freedom, personhood, and happiness.)

Consider the four conditions as a whole. Despite the unanswered questions, they provide a useful initial characterization of what it is to lead a happy life. Each requirement is plausibly taken to be a necessary condition of leading a happy life, and jointly, the requirements certainly seem sufficient. Someone who meets them all is satisfying his important desires sufficiently often, and he enjoys satisfying these desires; moreover, in satisfying the desires, he is realizing one or more "empirical selves" that he is "standing by," and he enjoys this self-realization. He has an "affirmative attitude" toward his life because he thinks that he is satisfying those important desires sufficiently often and that what he desires is worthy of desire. Moreover, what he desires *is* worthy of desire. Surely, this person is leading a happy life.

So much for the *initial* characterization of leading a happy life. The key to the second account of leading a happy life lies in the concept of enjoyment, for that concept mediates the conceptual connections among happiness, freedom, and personhood. The reason is that a special form of enjoyment is the central component of a happy life. The specialness of this form of enjoyment consists in the way it involves one's ability to act freely. The analysis of what it is to have this ability provides the basis for developing the picture of what it is to be a person, the picture that underlies the definition of happiness developed in Chapter 5. Chapter 2 is devoted to the discussion of freedom; Chapter 3, to personhood. Chapter 1 is devoted to an essential preliminary—arguing that thoughts can, in and of themselves, be motives for action. This argument yields an essential clarification of the notion of desire.

1 Kantian Motivation

Plato, Aristotle, and Kant share, in their philosophical psychology, a fundamentally important distinction between kinds of desires: between desires that depend on a person's conceptions in a special and fundamental way and desires that do not so depend on conceptions. Contemporary philosophical psychology also emphasizes the distinction. Stuart Hampshire, for example, remarks in *Freedom of the Individual* that "it is of first importance to this inquiry that the conception of an act or activity—and in some cases even the precise words in which the conception presents itself—can be the determining factor in the formation of a desire to act"; he adds, "This Don Quixotism [*sic*] is perfectly human, and has no place in the behavior of animals."[1] The importance of the distinc-

---

1. Stuart Hampshire, *Freedom of the Individual*, expanded ed. (Princeton, N.J.: Princeton University Press, 1975), p. 47. Another example is N. J. H. Dent, *The Moral Psychology of the Virtues* (Cambridge: Cambridge University Press, 1984), esp. chap. 4. Dent does not use the term 'conception-dependent' but the underlying ideas are essentially the same. It would not be far off the mark to view the distinction, as it figures in contemporary philosophical psychology, as a modern version of Aristotle's distinction between rational and arational desires. See, for example, David Wiggins, "Deliberation and Practical Reason," and "Weakness of the Will, Commensurability, and the Objects of Deliberation and Desire," in Amelie Rorty, ed., *Essays on Aristotle's Ethics* (Berkeley: University of California Press, 1980); Terence Irwin, "Aristotle on Reason, Desire, and Virtue," *Journal of Philosophy*, 72, no. 17 (2 October 1975), and idem, "Reason and Responsibility in Aristotle," in Rorty, *Essays on Aristotle's Ethics*.

tion between the two kinds of desires derives from the different ways in which they respond to reasoning.[2] Reasoning can readily eliminate (and even create) conception-dependent desires precisely because of the special way in which such desires depend on conceptions. Reasoning can also eliminate (and create) conception-independent desires—but not in the same way and not nearly so readily. This difference makes the distinction fundamental to any explanation of the relation between motivation and reason: our Don Quixoteism is essential to our rationality.

But exactly how is the distinction to be drawn? Kant is the best guide. For Kant, the conception-dependent desires are supplied by reason in its practical employment and are judgments: specifically, judgments that this or that action is sanctioned by the Categorical Imperative. Such desires are conception-dependent in the sense that they depend on the conceptions articulated in the judgment: if one did not have the judgment involving those conceptions, one would not have the desire; the desire, after all, is the judgment. The conception-independent desires are, for Kant, those that have their origin not in practical reason but in our animal nature.

I will argue for a generalized and modified version of this Kantian position. I will identify conception-dependent desires with thoughts that serve as desires; thus such desires need not be judgments (a fortiori, they need not be judgments about what the Categorical Imperative sanctions). Unlike Kant, I do not identify conception-dependent desires with desires supplied by the faculty of reason or by any other source. Being conception-dependent has nothing to do with any particular sort of origin. A similar point holds for conception-independent desires; I will identify them simply as those desires that are not thoughts; thus, contrary to Kant, conception-independent desires need not have their origin in our animal nature (although the typical examples of such desires will have such an origin).

The thesis that thoughts can be desires may seem paradoxical (at best!). Why accept such a conception of motivation? It is not as if there were no rival conceptions—the most obvious rival being a Humean conception of motivation (a conception I will characterize

2. Hampshire argues that the distinction between conception-dependent/independent desires is essential to ordinary psychological explanation. *Freedom of the Individual*, p. 50.

in detail later). My claim is that only the choice of Kantian conception allows us to draw adequately the fundamentally important distinction between conception-dependent and conception-independent desires. In addition, the choice between a Kantian or a Humean conception of motivation conditions one's picture of such philosophically central concepts as freedom and personhood. It is the Kantian conception that underlies the accounts of freedom and personhood given in the chapters that follow.

Before I argue for the Kantian conception, let me explain more fully what that conception is, beginning with an illustration of what I mean by the claim that a thought can serve as a desire. Imagine that Jones is contemplating quitting his job and sailing alone around the world. He is entranced by the thought of himself as a solo circumnavigator, and this thought serves as a desire to sail single-handed around the world. The thought in question is not one that Jones could fully and adequately express simply by saying 'I could sail around the world alone.' 'The' thought is actually a complex of thoughts that together constitute Jones's idea of what it would be like to be a solo circumnavigator. It is this complex that serves as the desire. The complex need not consist of verbalized thoughts or even of thoughts that Jones *could* fully or adequately verbalize. Some or all of the thoughts may be realized in images; thus part of Jones's complex may consist of his image of himself sailing under blue skies across halcyon seas.

Using the word 'conception' in a somewhat technical sense, let us call such a complex of thoughts a 'conception'. A conception may consist of any number of thoughts; there is no upper bound. As a lower bound, it is convenient to allow a single thought to count as a conception, even though, typically, a conception consists of several thoughts. A final note: the thoughts that constitute conceptions need not be *beliefs*; they may be the mere entertaining of an idea. I am using 'thought' to cover both cases; however, I will, in what follows, generally focus on the belief case.

Not every conception is a desire, of course. Smith and Jones may both have the same conception of what it would be like to sail around the world alone, but Smith, unlike Jones, need not desire to do so. However, the contrast to focus on here is not the contrast between conceptions that are or are not desires; rather, the crucial contrast is between conceptions that serve as desires and desires that are not conceptions. It has been clear at least since Aristotle's *Nicomachean Ethics* that some desires are not conceptions.[3] Sexual desire, a hungry person's desire for food, a thirsty person's desire for drink, and generally desires that Aristotle would ascribe to the arational part of the soul are not thoughts.[4] I take this for granted.

My proposal, as I noted above, is to identify conception-dependent desires with conceptions that serve as desires and to identify conception-independent desires with desires that are not conceptions. The idea is illustrated by the Jones example above. There is a clear sense in which Jones's desire for solo circumnavigation is conception-dependent: Jones would certainly not have that desire if he did not think of himself as single-handedly sailing around the world, for the thought *is* the desire. Nothing similar is true for conception-dependent desires since they are not thoughts. These proposed identifications are acceptable only if conception-desires—as I will provisionally call them—differ from nonconception-desires in being responsive to reasoning in a special way: in a way that gives reasoning a special power to eliminate (and create) such desires.

They do so differ. To see this, consider Jones's solo circumnavigation again. Jones, in preparation for his voyage, begins to read extensively about sailing and especially about storms at sea. Before he began reading, he had one collection of thoughts—call it C—that constituted his conception of what it would be like to sail around the world. C included the thought that solo circumnavi-

3. I would also argue that Plato and Aristotle held that thoughts can be desires. In addition to appetite and passion, both Plato and Aristotle distinguish a third kind of desire—rational desire (*boulesis*). It is not out of the question to interpret *boulesis* as a thought serving as a desire. In the *Metaphysics* (trans. W. D. Ross, 2d ed. [Oxford: Oxford University Press, 1928]), for example, Aristotle says: " ... the object of desire and the object of thought are the same. For the apparent good is the object of appetite (*epithumeton*) and the real good is the primary object of rational wish (*bouleton*). But desire is consequent on opinion rather than opinion on desire; for thinking is the starting point" (1972a26–30). One way to interpret this passage is to think of *boulesis* as a kind of thinking that is the starting point of action. Aristotle is not always as clear about this as one might wish (even though he is committed to the position that thought can by itself cause motion since that is what the unmoved mover does). Compare the *Nicomachean Ethics*, 1139a30–1139b5; and *De Anima*, Book III, chap. 10.

4. Compare Hampshire, *Freedom of the Individual*, p. 37: "Wanting—unlike, for example, regretting is not essentially thought-dependent.... Desire presupposes only the capacity to act and to feel."

gation was never life-threatening, a thought that was realized in the image of sailing under blue skies, masterfully guiding a boat across sedate seas. The information he gains by reading leads him to form a new conception, C^*. C^* includes the thought that the ocean can be hostile and life-threatening, and the dominant image is of Jones, cold, wet, and afraid, struggling with out-of-control sails under dark clouds on a black sea. He no longer desires to sail around the world. That desire disappeared when his conception changed, for the old conception C *was* the desire, and the new conception C^* is not one that has the power to motivate Jones. (I will later take up the question of why some conceptions serve as desires while others do not.) The point to emphasize here is that Jones's change of conception is the result of thinking and reasoning. Jones reasons that, if the information about storms is correct, his original conception C is highly inaccurate and incomplete; since he believes the information about storms, he revises his conception. Of course, such a change in conception need not be the result of thinking and reasoning. My point is simply that thinking and reasoning *can* change conceptions by revealing them to be false, inaccurate, incomplete, or faulty in some other way.

In general, conceptions that serve as desires are *intrinsically* responsive to reasoning. An essential feature of reasoning is that it can alter our conceptions of things. Thoughts are (perhaps not the only, but certainly paramount among) the inputs and outputs of the mental process that is reasoning; a process that lacked the power to alter our thoughts would not be reasoning. So conceptions—as complexes of thoughts—are *intrinsically* the sort of thing that reasoning can alter. It alters them by showing them to be false, incomplete, unrealistic, or in some other way faulty (we do not need a complete catalogue of the ways here). This makes the desires provided by our conceptions intrinsically responsive to reason, for when reason eliminates the conception that provides the desire, it *thereby* eliminates the desire—the desire *being* the conception. (To avoid too much emphasis on the elimination of desire, we should note that reasoning can also readily create conception-desires; however, we will have to wait until later to see that this is so.)

Nonconception-desires, on the other hand, are only *extrinsically* responsive to reasoning. Such desires can be eliminated by reasoning, but there is no intrinsic tie to reasoning. Consider an example:

I have a nonconception desire for another bottle of wine; however, I reason from facts about my host's demeanor to the conclusion that another bottle is not forthcoming. To make the best of a poor situation, I decide to turn my attention away from my desire for wine and let myself become deeply involved in the conversation, with the result that my desire for more wine disappears. Had I not reasoned, the desire would have persisted. Nonetheless, even though reasoning can in the way illustrated eliminate nonconception-desires, it is not essential to reasoning's being reasoning that it have the power to eliminate such desires. In fact, desires that are not conceptions are typically resistant to elimination by reasoning: lust, hunger, and thirst can easily survive the demonstration of their futility or unreasonableness.

So much for illustration. I must admit that this picture of ourselves as possessing motives intrinsically responsive to reasoning strikes me as both attractive and important. The capacity to eliminate (and create) such motives through thinking and reasoning gives us a certain mastery over ourselves—a mastery that allows reason to shape our lives by shaping our motives instead of having our lives dominated by motives that lie outside the dominion of reason. This sort of mastery is "perfectly human, and has no place in the behavior of animals." But this Kantian picture of motivation depends on the thesis—for many, the at-best paradoxical thesis— that thoughts can be desires. Doesn't this dependence render the picture not only unattractive but patently false? I do not think so. I will argue for the thesis by arguing against three objections; the answers to the objections will elicit the positive argument for the thesis.

The first objection turns on the fact that what motivates the thesis is the need to draw a distinction between conception-dependent and conception-independent desires. The objection is that there are simpler, less controversial ways of drawing the relevant distinction; we do not need the thesis that conceptions can be desires.

The second objection is that the thesis conflicts with what would seem to be an indisputable feature of the concept desire. To see this feature, consider states like hunger and thirst. These states are or involve desires: the desire to eat and the desire to drink. Indeed, one cannot count as hungry or thirsty without the relevant desire. It is not coherent to describe a state as hunger and also suppose that this very state can sometimes be (or involve) a desire and sometimes not. One might contend that this illustrates a general feature of the notion of desire: being a desire is an essential property of a state. But if the word 'desire' denotes an essential property, conceptions cannot be desires; the claim that conceptions can be desires is the claim that conceptions are on occasion but not always desires. So if being a desire is an essential property of a state, the thesis that conceptions can be desires must be wrong.

The third objection can be put as a question: even if being a desire is not an essential property, what possible ground could we ever have for holding that conceptions can be desires? Thought and desire are different kinds of psychological states, with different explanatory roles in ordinary psychological explanation. So if to explain a person's thought and action, we need to attribute not just a certain thought or thoughts to him but a certain desire as well, don't we thereby have grounds for attributing to him two states, each with its *distinct* explanatory role?

Hampshire on Desire

I will answer the first objection by considering the way in which Hampshire in *Freedom of the Individual* draws the distinction between conception-dependent and conception-independent desires. His discussion represents the most plausible way of drawing the distinction without recourse to the thesis that conceptions can be desires. Two terminological points: first, although Hampshire uses the word 'conception' in roughly the sense we are using it, he does not explicitly stipulate that a conception is a complex of thoughts. This slight difference should cause no problem. Also, he often refers to conception-dependent desires as desires *mediated by descriptions*. For our purposes, we can regard the two ways of describing the desires as equivalent. Indeed, Hampshire explains that "The mediating description represents the subject's conception of the object, or activity, desired."[5]

The place to begin is with Hampshire's claim that "we can distinguish between cases in which the conception of the activity is essential to the existence of the desire from cases in which it is

5. Ibid., p. 46

accidental.''[6] There are two features by virtue of which we can draw the distinction. First, there is, in the case of conception-dependent desires, a systematic connection between the conception, the origin of the desire, and the content of the desire. Hampshire offers the example of Smith, who wants to buy the most expensive picture in the gallery. He distinguishes two possibilities:

> It might be the case that Smith had conceived of the desire of buying whatever picture happened to be the most expensive picture in the gallery. Or he might have seen a picture, which he immediately liked and wanted, and which happened to be the most expensive. In the second case, his desire is unmediated by this, or any other description of the picture: in the first case the desire to buy the picture is mediated by the description, *which is essential to the desire, and specifies the exact nature of the desire.* The two desires are entirely different and reveal very different characters; but the same form of words may truthfully represent both situations.[7]

The connection between conception, origin, and content can be put counterfactually: if it were not for Smith's conception of himself as buying the most expensive painting in the gallery, he would not have the desire to buy the most expensive painting in the gallery.

The second feature turns on the way in which a conception may be involved not in the origin but in the continued existence of a desire:

> A mediating description may be highly specific, and may exactly determine the nature of the action or activity desired; or the conception, on which the existence of the desire depends, may be a relatively vague conception of the activity desired. In either case, *that particular desire to act would disappear, if the conception were shown to be in some way faulty or confused or unreal.* Whatever the character of the conception, general or specific, vague or precise, having the desire may depend on having the conception as its necessary condition.[8]

Again, the point can be put counterfactually, as Hampshire himself does: "that particular desire to act would disappear, if the conception were shown to be in some way faulty or confused or unreal."

6. Ibid.
7. Ibid., my emphasis.
8. Ibid., p. 47, my emphasis.

For example, it could be true that Smith's desire to buy the most expensive painting in the gallery would disappear if he were to discover that there is no such thing. For example, he might find that the paintings are being given away for free or that they are not really paintings but holographic projections.

The idea, then, is to distinguish between conception-dependent and conception-independent desires as follows:

> (*) A desire D is conception-dependent if and only if there is some conception such that one would not have formed D if one had not had that conception, and D would disappear if that conception were shown to be in some way faulty, confused, or unreal.

In fairness to Hampshire, I should note that he does not explicitly formulate anything like (*), and it may well be that his remarks are merely intended to draw attention to a distinction without offering any specific definition. However, a good deal of the philosophical psychology literature seems to rely implicitly (and certainly uncritically) on (*)—or conditions essentially like (*)—to draw the sort of distinction between desires that Hampshire is after.[9] For this reason, I want to focus on (*). If (*) is acceptable, there is, of course, no need to resort to the idea that conceptions *are* desires.

But (*) is not acceptable. The problem is that every desire turns out to be conception-dependent. Consider the desire to eat, one of Hampshire's paradigm cases of a conception-independent desire: "the desire of the hungry man for food, or of the thirsty man for drink, and some desires that arise from other bodily needs, may come into existence independently of any conception."[10] There are three cases to distinguish.

1. Seeing the steak on the table, I form a desire to eat it. Now steak happens to be the only thing I am hungry for: that is, I would not have formed the desire to eat what I saw if I had not conceived of it as steak; if that conception were to prove faulty, confused, or unreal, the desire would disappear. Thus the desire to eat to eat what I see on the table is conception-dependent according to (*).

---

9. See, for example, Dent, *The Moral Psychology of the Virtues*, esp. chap. 4.
10. Hampshire, *Freedom of the Individual*, p. 36.

2. When I see the steak and form the desire to eat it, I am so hungry that I would eat almost anything—that is, anything I regard as edible. It is still true that I would not have formed the desire to eat what I saw if I had not conceived of it as edible, and if that conception were to prove faulty, confused, or unreal, the desire would disappear. Again, the desire to eat what I see on the table is conception-dependent.

3. It may seem as if there is a third case: I see the steak and form a desire that I could express by saying, "I want to eat *that*"—where 'that' is not in any way elliptical for 'that steak,' 'that edible thing,' or any other completion of 'that . . .'. Hampshire at one point describes cases such as this, as cases in which "I merely look and want." He claims that such desires presuppose just "the capacity to act and feel," not the capacity to form conceptions.[11] This desire is—it would seem—conception-independent.

Or is it? It depends on what we mean by 'conception'. The question to ask is: what is required for a creature to count as desiring to eat? To have the desire to eat is, at least, to be disposed to ingest what one identifies or discriminates as edible. Some kind of identification or discrimination is essential; this is not to say that self-conscious classification of objects as edible is required to count as having the desire to eat but merely that we must be able to describe the creature as discriminating, not necessarily in a self-conscious way, between the edible and the nonedible. A creature surely does not count as wanting to *eat* if it indiscriminately ingests whatever it finds—rocks, dirt, and plastic—as readily as food. We could perhaps describe it as desiring to ingest but not as desiring to eat. A disordered creature might be moved to such behavior by its desire to eat, but even in this case we count it as wanting to eat because normally, the desire moves it to eat what it identifies as edible.

Now, on one way of reading 'conception' it is enough to qualify as having a conception of the edible that one have a capacity for discrimination that plays an appropriate role in guiding behavior. If we understand 'conception' in this way, my desire to eat in case 3 is conception-dependent. If I did not have the conception of the steak as edible, I would (insofar as I was not disordered) not desire

11. Ibid.

to eat it; if that conception were to prove faulty—for example, I discovered the "steak" was plastic—the desire would (insofar as I was not disordered) disappear.

Similar remarks can be made about any purportedly conception-independent desire; it would seem that they are all conception-dependent. One might hope to avoid this result by distinguishing two senses of 'conception'. One might insist that there is a sense of 'conception' on which having a conception is tied to being a language user: one counts as having a conception only if one can articulate that conception in language.[12] In this sense of 'conception', mere identification or discrimination is not enough to qualify as having a conception. One could claim that (*) does not hold in case 3 for this sense of 'conception'.

But this does not help. (*) is intended to draw a distinction between two kinds of desires. However, the present suggestion grants that (*) holds for both kinds of desires—although in different senses of 'conception'. To grant this is to grant that (*) fails to delineate what is truly distinctive of the two kinds of desires, for both stand in *exactly the same sort* of relations to conceptions. It is just that in one case the conceptions are not essentially tied to language and in the other case they are. What the suggestion really does is draw a line between language-dependent and language-independent desires. No doubt there is such a line to be drawn, but it is not the same as the conception-dependent/independent distinction. That distinction is intended to capture a fundamental difference in susceptibility to reason; there is no reason to think that the language-dependent/independent distinction captures such a difference.

Another way to avoid the problems with (*) would be to abandon it. That is, one might suggest replacing (*) in favor of distinguishing between desires in terms of their origin: for example, between desires that arise out of, or in some way owe their existence to, bodily needs (desires like hunger and thirst); and desires that arise out of, or in some way owe their existence to, thinking and reasoning. Again, there is certainly such a distinction to be drawn, but it is not the same as the conception-dependent/independent distinction, for the distinction in terms of origin does not capture any important

12. This would appear to be Hampshire's position.

difference in susceptibility to reasoning. For example, hunger may, and typically does, owe its existence to a bodily need; yet it can nonetheless be eliminated by reasoning. For example, as Smith is about to open the refrigerator to eat a piece of pie, he forces himself to reflect on the already quite noticeable bulge around his waist and on the fact that he has been telling himself for over a year that buying pants with a size thirty-six waist is only temporary until he loses weight. Admitting these facts, he reasons his way to the conclusion that the waist size will indeed be temporary—a temporary step on the way to size thirty-eight—unless he stops eating. In the midst of his guilt and new-found resolve to lose weight, his hunger disappears.

To summarize: the point of drawing the conception-dependence/ independence distinction is to capture a fundamental difference in susceptibility to reasoning. But each of the above distinctions—be it (*), the language-dependence idea, or the distinction in terms of origin—fails to capture the difference in question. Now, the first objection was that we can distinguish between kinds of desires without committing ourselves to the thesis that conceptions can be desires. However, it appears that no such way to draw the distinction exists. This constitutes a strong case for the thesis that conceptions can be desires, for the distinction in question must be a part of any plausible picture of the relation between reason and motivation.

But what of the other two objections? Let us turn to the second one.

Two Kinds of Desire

The second objection is, in brief, that desire in an essential property. In answer, I grant that 'desire' sometimes denotes an essential property. However, I contend that there are two senses of 'desire', one in which it denotes an essential property and one in which it does not. For clarity, some new terminology is needed to replace the conception-dependent/independent terminology, which, for all its initially useful suggestiveness, is misleading since it suggests a distinction in terms of some sort of counterfactual dependence on conceptions, and this is not really the nature of the distinction at all.

The first thing we need is a general term for the entire class of desires, the class that includes both of the distinct kinds of desire. We could simply use 'desire', but since, on my view, that term may denote either of the two kinds of desire, some other expression would serve better. 'Motive' is as good as any. By 'motive'—that is, a desire in general—I mean a state that plays a certain role in commonsense psychological explanation and justification of thought and action. There is no need to characterize this role fully, but it is worth noting a few features. Motives cause action—but not always: we can have motives on which we do not act; they also typically cause a certain kind of thinking—looking for a way to do what one is motivated to do; motives vary in intensity, and the greater the intensity, the more likely—as a rule—it is that the motive will cause action; finally, motives play a role in justification: indeed, as I will argue later, a motive is—other things being equal—a justification for action.

Now, turning to the two kinds of desire, let us say that a state S is a desire, *in the strict sense*, that p if and only if necessarily, every token of S is a motive to bring it about that p.[13] In other words, to be a desire in the strict sense, every (actual and possible) token of the state must have a certain motivational force.[14] I will call such states 'S-desires' ('S' for 'strict'). Being a motive is an essential property of an S-desire.

13. This definition is correct only if we understand the state S to be of "lowest psychological type": S is of lowest psychological type if and only if S is a token of a psychological state but no token of S has (or could have) tokens. Otherwise, every desire is an S-desire since every desire is a token of the state of being a motive, and every token of being a motive is a motive. (I am indebted to David Copp for this objection.) The "lowest psychological type" requirement avoids this problem since being a motive is not a state of lowest psychological type. Given the weight placed on it, the type/token distinction (with respect to desires and beliefs) merits a brief illustration. Suppose Smith and Jones both desire to vacation on Hawaii. There is a sense in which they do not have the same desire; Smith's desire could exist even if Jones's did not and vice versa. But there is also a sense in which they both do have the same desire: they both desire to vacation on Hawaii. (Smith desires *his* vacationing on Hawaii; Jones, *his*—i.e., *Jones's*—vacationing on Hawaii; but vacationing on Hawaii is what they both desire.) I will express these facts by saying that Smith and Jones instantiate different tokens of the desire-type, vacationing on Hawaii. Similarly, if they both believe that a vacation on Hawaii would be pleasant, they have different tokens of the same belief-type.

14. There is no circularity to worry about here. It would be circular to try to define 'desire' in terms of motive, but that is not what I am doing. I am distinguishing kinds of desires, not defining 'desire' itself.

In what follows, I will identify conception-independent desires with S-desires. However, first it is worth noting that philosophical talk of desires has frequently been talk of S-desires. Hume, for example, thinks that "propensities" or "aversions" must be present in every action, where a propensity or an aversion is, for Hume, clearly a state every instance of which has a motivational force. One cannot have a propensity for (or an aversion to) eating ice cream without having a motive to eat (or avoid eating) ice cream. Furthermore, when Plato and Aristotle talk of appetite (*epithumia*) and passion (*thumos*), they are talking of states that one cannot instantiate without being motivated to act in certain ways. Plato gives thirst and hunger as prime examples of appetites, and one cannot be thirsty or hungry without having a motive to drink or eat.[15] Anger is the prime example of passion, and anger involves, according to Aristotle, a motive for revenge.[16] In one way, these examples are somewhat misleading in that they are all examples of appetites or passions, and nothing in the definition of S-desires entails that they must be either appetites or passions. However, I suggest that in us—in human beings—S-desires are typically (but perhaps not always) appetites and passions. This is a contingent fact about us.

Philosophers have sometimes recognized states that serve as desires without being S-desires—without being such that every token of such a state serves as a motive. Let us call these desires in the extended sense: 'E-desires', for short. So an E-desire is a *token* of a state-type, where *that token* is a motive but where not every token of that state-type is a motive.[17] Kant is one obvious example of a philosopher who has recognized the existence of E-desires; among contemporary philosophers, Thomas Nagel is another. Both think that judgments (of certain special sorts) sometimes serve as motives; however, they both recognize that it is not always the case that a token of the relevant sort of judgment has motive force.[18]

15. *Republic*, Book IV, 437f.
16. See, for example, the *Nicomachean Ethics*, Book VII, chap. 6.
17. Again, the state-type must be of lowest psychological type.
18. For Nagel's position, see Thomas Nagel, *The Possibility of Altruism* (New York: Oxford University Press, 1970), pp. 110–111. As for Kant, some claim that he abandons the position that a judgment can, in and of itself, be a motive when he introduces the notion of respect as a feeling. But consider this passage from the *Grundlegung*: "respect . . . means merely the consciousness of the submission of my

The thesis that conceptions can be desires can now be restated as the thesis that conceptions can be E-desires. These are the conception-dependent desires; the conception-independent desires are the S-desires. This is consistent with our earlier identification of conception-independent desires with desires that are not conceptions. S-desires cannot be conceptions since desire cannot be an essential property of a conception.

Introducing the terminology of E-desires does not, of course, answer the second objection. For all that I have said so far, it is possible that there are no E-desires. I need to show that there are, or at least that there could be, E-desires. To this end, I will argue, first, that this thesis could be true—that it is not false a priori. This answers the second objection; it shows that there is a sense of 'desire' on which desire is not an essential property. Next, I will argue that there are in fact E-desires. This will provide an answer to the third and last objection, which was that we could never have good explanatory grounds for thinking that conceptions serve as desires.

The Humean Thesis

I will begin by distinguishing between unstructured and structured motives. An unstructured motive may consist of a single psychological state, or it may be a combination of such states; the defining features of an unstructured motive is that it is a motive no part of which is a motive. A motive consisting of a single psychological state satisfies this condition because, as a *single* psychological state, it has no *part* that could be a motive. But a collection of psychological states may also satisfy the condition. To take an especially relevant example, a conception—a complex of thoughts—counts as an unstructured motive, provided that, while the complex as a whole is a motive, no part of the complex is a motive. Not every motive is unstructured; for example, one may desire to play chess and believe that if Paul comes over, he will play. This desire/

---

will to a law without the intervention of other influences on my mind. The direct determination of my will by the law and the consciousness of this determination is respect" (my emphasis): *Foundations of the Metaphysics of Morals*, trans. Lewis White Beck (1959; reprint, Indianapolis: Bobbs-Merrill, 1980), p. 17 n.2. Compare *The Critique of Practical Reason*, Book I, Chap. 3, in which there appears to be grounds for the charge that Kanta abandons the position that judgments can, in and of themselves, be motives.

belief combination may be a motive to invite Paul over, although neither the desire alone nor the belief alone is such a motive. The combination has a motive (the desire) as a part so it is not an unstructured motive. Let us call motives that consist of a motive as a part 'structured motives'. Frequently, when we ask, "What was his motive?" we are seeking a structured motive. For example: "What was his motive in lying to the police?" "He wanted to protect his son and believed that he had to lie to do so." But it is part of commonsense psychological explanation to recognize unstructured motives. Indeed, the belief/desire pair in the example just given would not be a structured motive if it did not consist of the unstructured motive provided by the desire to protect the son.

Many will reject the claim that a conception, just on its own, can be an E-desire—the claim that a belief can be an unstructured motive for action. They will do so because they hold what I call the 'Humean Thesis':

(1) Only an S-desire can be an unstructured motive.
(2) A belief (or any other psychological state that is not an S-desire) can be part of a structured motive only if another part of the motive is an S-desire.

Note that 'desire' must be understood in the strict sense in (1). If 'desire' just means "motive" (desire in general), (1) simply asserts that unstructured motives must be motives. Those who hold the Humean Thesis are not making this trivial claim; they intend their claim to be inconsistent with the claim that beliefs can be unstructured motives.[19]

One might object that the Humean need not understand 'desire' in the strict sense in (1). Why should he not ignore the E-desire/S-

19. This, indeed, seems to be what Hume himself has in mind. He holds that a "propensity" or an "aversion" must be present in every action; as I pointed out earlier, Humean propensities and aversions are states such that one cannot be in them without being motivated in some particular way: in short, they are S-desires. Moreover, Hume argues that "it can never in the least concern us to know that such objects are causes, and such others effects, if both the causes and effects be indifferent to us. Where the objects themselves do not affect us, their connexion can never give them any influence." David Hume, *A Treatise of Human Nature*, ed. L. A. Selby-Bigge (Oxford: Oxford University Press, 1978), p. 414. I take this to mean that a belief never motivates without the addition of an appropriate "propensity" or "aversion." In short, Hume holds both (1) and (2).

desire distinction entirely and simply say that by 'desire' he means (a) an attitude that is not a belief but which (b) typically combines with beliefs to cause action? The problem with this suggestion is that it does not uniquely describe desires. Hopes, fears, worries, and various sorts of emotions also combine with beliefs to cause action. So what is definitive of the Humean notion of a desire? I suggest that the notion of an S-desire identifies the defining feature of a fundamental sort of motivational state—that feature being that every possible token of the state is a motive. It is worth pointing out here that understanding 'desire' in the strict sense in (1) does not mean being ungenerous about what counts as a desire. As Bernard Williams points out, 'desire' should, in the context of Humean theories of motivation, be understood as including "such things as dispositions of evaluation, patterns of emotional reaction, personal loyalties, and various projects, as they may be abstractly called, embodying commitments of the agent."[20] I would only point out that, if the Humean Thesis is not to be rendered trivial, the items mentioned must be, or must include as an essential component, an S-desire.

The claim that conceptions can be E-desires will win general acceptance only if I can produce convincing reasons for abandoning the Humean Thesis. The place to being is with the claim that the thesis is a priori. Many hold this view; they just cannot see how the thesis could be false.

To see how it could be false, suppose that we are demigods and that we decide to create some creatures. The creatures will have to live in a very hostile environment, so we decided to make them very aggressive; however, we do not want the creatures to be so aggressive that they kill one another. There are two ways we can curb their aggressiveness. One way conforms to the Humean Thesis. We can build in each creature an S-desire not to kill members of its own kind. The desire and the belief "this is a member my own kind" constitute a structured motive not to kill that member.

Imagine that we are about to design a creature in this way, when it dawns on one of us that there is an alternative. She points out that the proposed creature will have a central nervous system; part

---

20. Bernard Williams, "Internal and External Reasons," in *Moral Luck* (Cambridge: Cambridge University Press, 1981), p. 105.

of this system—the motor system—will govern the movement of its limbs. This motor system is a nonpsychological system; psychological states are among its input, but the system itself is the nonpsychological, physiological substructure that subserves the generation of behavior from psychological states. The suggestion is that we design the creature so that when it sees a member of its own kind, the possibility of nonaggression occurs to it; it thinks, "I could be friendly"—where this belief provides an input directly to its motor system. The input causes it to behave nonaggressively (e.g., the creature lowers its weapons and so on). No S-desire need combine with the belief for it to provide this input.

The following diagrams capture the contrast between the two ways of designing the creature.

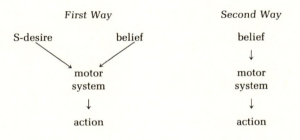

The first way provides two inputs to the motor system; the second, one.

In the second way of designing the creature, we may suppose that not every token of the belief functions as an unstructured motive. We design the creature so that when it is attacked by one of its own kind (something that happens when a creature becomes disordered), it has no motive of any sort to be nonaggressive. It still believes "I could be friendly," but that belief is—as is certainly possible with any belief—motivationally completely inert; it provides no input whatsoever to the creature's motor system. It follows that the belief "I could be friendly" is not an S-desire even when it serves as an unstructured motive. The belief is an E-desire: a conception that serves as a motive.[21] (To keep things simple, I have

---

21. There is an objection here: what if whenever the belief serves as a unstructured

taken a case in which the conception consists of a single belief.) One might object here that, in the second way of designing the creature, it is unclear that the belief "I could be friendly" qualifies as a *motive*. After all, is the direct connection between the belief and the motor system compatible with the behavior being intentional or goal directed? If not, why think of the belief as a motive? It should quiet these qualms to elaborate a bit on the psychology of the creature. Suppose that even when the creature is not under attack, it does not automatically lower its weapons when, upon seeing a member of its own kind, it believes "I could be friendly." Rather, if it takes itself to have a sufficiently strong justification for aggressive behavior (if, for example, it realizes that the other creature is stealing its food), it overrides its impulse to be friendly and attacks instead. When it lacks any such justification for aggressive behavior, the creature (if not under attack) takes the motive provided by "I could be friendly" as a sufficient justification for friendly behavior, and the impulse to be friendly is effective in producing such behavior. We could continue to elaborate along these lines, but it is not necessary. The point is that such systematic relations between belief, behavior, and justification should be enough for the belief to qualify as a motive.

A Humean might grant that we have said enough to show that the belief can qualify as a motive, but he might object that, in constructing the creature so that the belief is a motive, we have tacitly given it an S-desire not to kill. After all, the creature is so constructed that it has a standing disposition not to kill. Isn't such a disposition an S-desire? Every token of such a disposition is a motive. In answer, note that this objection grants that the thought "I could be friendly" is the only nondispositional state that serves as a motive not to kill. *And this is to grant the Kantian view.* The argument between the Kantian and the Humean is over what *non*-dispositional states serve as motives. The Humean contends that a nondispositional S-desire is required; the Kantian denies this. A Humeanism that grants that the thought is the only nondispositional state that serves as a motive is not a "Humeanism" with which I have any argument.

---

motive not to kill, it also counts as a token of the S-desire not to kill? Then the belief would not be an E-desire—would not be an E-desires that is not an S-desire. I answer this objection in note 23.

It is clear that we could construct the creature in either of the two ways we have described, and this shows that the Humean Thesis is not a priori since that thesis is not true of the creature constructed in the second way. But, of course, showing that the thesis is not true a priori is not the same as showing that it is not true. Isn't there reason to think it is true? Won't the best explanation of why a person is motivated in this way or that be—just as a matter of empirical fact—an explanation that posits S-desires to account for motivation? I do not think so. On the contrary, the best explanation of certain facts about action treats certain conceptions as E-desires. Let us call this claim the 'Kantian Thesis'.

The Kantian Thesis

What facts about action support the Kantian Thesis? No examples uncontroversially support it; it is a question of how the facts are best explained. Consider the following example:

> George, who has just taken his Ph.D. in chemistry, finds it extremely difficult to get a job. He is not very robust in health, which cuts down the number of jobs he might be able to do satisfactorily. His wife has to go out to work to keep them, which itself causes a great deal of strain, since they have small children and there are severe problems about looking after them. The results of all this, especially on the children, are damaging. An older chemist, who knows about the situation, says that he can get George a decently paid job in a certain laboratory, which pursues research in chemical and biological warfare. George says he cannot accept this, since he is opposed to chemical and biological warfare. The older man replies that he is not too keen on it himself, come to that, but after all George's refusal is not going to make the job or the laboratory go away; what is more, he happens to know that if George refuses the job, it will certainly go to a contemporary of George's who is not inhibited by any such scruples and is likely, if appointed, to push along the research with greater zeal than George would. Indeed, it is not merely concern for George and his family, but (to speak frankly and in confidence) some alarm about this other man's excess of zeal, which led the older man to offer to use his influence to get George the job. . . . George's wife, to whom he is deeply attached, has views (the details of which need not concern us) from which it follows that at least there is nothing particularly wrong with research into CBW.[22]

22. The example is Bernard Williams's, in J. J. C. Smart and Bernard Williams,

Imagine that George does refuse the job. His motive is not his opposition to chemical and biological warfare (CBW) research. The
older chemist makes it clear to him that, by refusing, he is furthering
such research. What George achieves is *his* not participating in such
research; he ensures that he remains true to a certain conception.
The complex of thoughts that constitutes this conception includes
the thought "I do not (knowingly and willingly) engage in CBW
research" and the thought realized in George's image of himself as
taking a lonely stand against the tide of social injustice. George
pictures himself alone, beset on one side by the indifferent masses;
on the other, by ruthless corporate giants.

What I will call the 'Kantian explanation' of George's refusal does
not deny that George can be described as desiring that he not engage
in CBW research. The issue is whether it is an S-desire or an E-
desire. The Kantian explanation opts for the second alternative,
identifying George's conception as an unstructured motive that
George has for refusing. This explanation of George's refusal is
attractive for its simplicity and economy. After all, what George
achieves by his refusal is his remaining true to a certain conception
of himself. What objection is there to assigning this conception a
role as an unstructured motive?

A Humean objection.   A Humean will think there is an obvious
objection. He will not deny that George's conception plays a key
motivational role; it is obvious that it does. But the Humean asks
how the motivational role of this conception is to be explained and
answers that an appeal to an appropriate S-desire is necessary. The
combination of that desire and the conception constitute the structured motive George has for refusing the job. It is easy to think of
appropriate S-desires. For example, George may simply S-desire
not to be someone who researches into CBW, and he may S-desire
this more strongly than he S-desires anything else.

This objection may appear powerful, but it is easy to turn the
tables. The first step is to ask for the Humean's explanation of
George's S-desiring, for example, not to be someone who engages
in the relevant sort of research. The zealous researcher—the one

Utilitarianism: For and Against (Cambridge: Cambridge University Press, 1973), pp.
97–98.

who takes the job when George does not—has no such desire, so why does George? Of course, it is not hard to see how the Humean might explain the posited S-desire. For example, he might appeal to George's upbringing and education as causal factors that play a central role in the formation of the desire. The zealous researcher was subject to different influences, so his desires are different. But the proponent of the Kantian Thesis can appeal to these same factors to explain directly—that is, without appeal to the Humean's posited desires—the fact that George's upbringing and education have led him to be motivated by the conception of himself as not engaging in CBW research. So the proponent of the Kantian Thesis can explain George's refusal and explain why George's conception is a motive. The Humean explains the motivational role of the conception too, but his account is unnecessarily complex: the posited desires are not really necessary since the Kantian Thesis yields a simpler and equally adequate explanation.[23]

One might object here that simplicity here is not only a matter of counting desires; it is a question of which thesis best fits in with our other beliefs and with other explanatory tasks. But the Kantian Thesis wins on this score too. The Humean must grant that we need to draw the distinction between conception-independent and conception-dependent desires, and there would appear to be no satisfactory way to do this without recognizing that thoughts can serve as desires (E-desires). Moreover, as we will see in subsequent chapters, the thesis that thoughts can be desires is linked, in systematic and important ways, to the accounts of freedom, personhood, and happiness.

A second objection. There is another, deeper objection to consider. According to the Kantian, George is, while the zealous researcher is not, susceptible to motivation by certain sorts of conceptions. The Humean could point out that it is certainly implausible to suppose that there is no psychological explanation of

23. Now we are in a position to answer the objection raised earlier in note 21: what if whenever a belief is a unstructured motive, it is also a token of an appropriate S-desire? Considerations of simplicity and economy argue against this suggestion. Why should we insist on thinking of a motivating belief as also an S-desire when seeing the belief as by itself an unstructured motive yields a perfectly adequate explanation? The insistence that the belief is an instance of an appropriate S-desire is just an ill-founded attempt to save the Humean Thesis.

why we are sometimes motivated and sometimes not be certain conceptions. Such susceptibility is, typically at least, in part the product of the possession and interaction of a variety of beliefs, desires, hopes, fears, ideals, and so on. Moreover, such a psychologically explained susceptibility is itself a psychological state and one that figures importantly in motivation. Indeed, conceptions only become motives when combined with such a susceptibility. But—the Humean continues—doesn't being susceptible in this sense amount to having an S-desire? After all, isn't susceptibility necessarily motivational? Consider the state-type *being susceptible to such-and-such kind of motivation*. Won't every token of such a type itself be a motive? If so, George's conception is not an unstructured motive but part of a structured motive—the other part being his susceptibility to certain kinds of motivation.

The answer to this objection is that not every state that inclines one to be motivated in a certain way need itself be a motive. The answer to the question "Doesn't the susceptibility amount to an S-desire?" is no; indeed, it is not a desire at all. Consider George. What explains his being motivated by his conception is that he is susceptible to motivation by conceptions that represent him as taking a lonely stand against the tide of social injustice. This susceptibility is a disposition to have unstructured motives of a certain sort, and it is perfectly coherent to hold that this disposition to form motives is not itself a motive. Indeed, it is not only coherent, it is part of ordinary psychological explanation; for having such motive-forming dispositions is part of having a certain character. Part of having a character is to be disposed to form certain motives—not because one has other motives but just because one is the sort of person that forms such motives.

A third objection.   The Humean may object that the above arguments show too much. If we can in some cases explain action in terms of motivating conceptions without any appeal to S-desires, why not in all cases? If the argument works in the case of George, doesn't it show that we could always eliminate reference to S-desires in favor of motivating beliefs? But this would be absurd. After all, there are S-desires. Hunger is, or involves, an S-desire to eat, and sometimes one's eating behavior is explained by one's hunger.

An adequate response must explain when Kantian explanation called for; and, when Humean. There are at least two features in the example of George that suggest the use of a Kantian explanation. The first is the 'motivational saliency' of George's conception. The Humean cannot plausibly deny that this conception plays a basic motivational role in George's refusal of the job. He differs from the Kantian only in insisting on a different explanation of why the conception has such a salient motivational role. The second feature is the lack of any motivationally salient S-desire. This is not to say that it is difficult to think of S-desires that might motivate George. George might S-desire to be a moral person, believe that being a moral person means not engaging in CBW research, believe that he could continue not to engage in CBW research, and so refuse the job. Or George might simply S-desire not to engage in CBW research, believe he could continue not to do so, and thus refuse the job. Or he might S-desire to win the respect of his friends, believe that not engaging in CBW research is a way to win their respect, believe that he could continue not to engage in such research, and thus refuse. But which of these S-desires is in fact the one that motivates George? None of them stands out as an obvious motivational factor in the way George's conception does.

One might object here that we could determine which S-desire motivates George by considering a wide enough range of George's behavior. We might, for example, have grounds to attribute the desire to be moral as opposed, say, to the desire to impress his friends, if the former desire played a role in explaining a wide range of behavior while the latter did not. But there is a problem here. Should we regard the desire to be moral as an S-desire or an E-desire? Since the Humean Thesis is not a priori, the Humean cannot just assume that it is an S-desire. What the Humean needs is both a way of determining which desire to posit and a reason for always taking the posited desire to be an S-desire. In the example of George, the Humean cannot satisfactorily meet this dual requirement.

It would be a mistake to suggest that these two features—saliency of the belief and lack of saliency of any S-desire—should be taken as a rule for choosing between the Kantian or the Humean explanation. They are just a guide. We should allow ourselves to take a variety of factors into account—the person's past, what he himself says about his beliefs and desires, and so on. All that is required is that, by taking a variety of factors into account, we are able case by case to decide between Kantian and Humean explanations in a way that yields useful and illuminating explanations of behavior. I see no reason to think we cannot do this.

This completes my argument that there are E-desires—conceptions that serve as unstructured motives. This Don Quixoteism is, as I remarked at the beginning, essential to understanding the connection between reason and motivation. We can further illustrate this point if we return to the earlier discussion of the notion of a susceptibility to motivation, for the fact that E-desires can be eliminated through thinking and reasoning provides one with a certain mastery over one's susceptibilities to motivation.

As an example of such mastery, consider George again. He is especially susceptible to motivation by conceptions that represent him as taking a lonely stand against the tide of social injustice, and he is motivated by such a conception to refuse the CBW research job. Imagine George having second thoughts about his position as he thinks about the effects that his refusing the job will have on his children. He finds himself wishing that he were not motivated to refuse, and he begins to think about what, in his mind, really constitutes a stand against social injustice. He concentrates on the effect of allowing the zealous researcher to take the job, and he arrives at the conclusion that to stand against social injustice, he must take, not refuse, the job. And he is motivated to take it— motivated by a conception that represents taking the job as a stand against social injustice. He is no longer motivated to refuse, for his motivation to refuse came from another conception, one that represented refusing as a stand against social injustice and he no longer subscribes to that conception of the matter. George is master of his susceptibility to motivation; his motives are not dictated by his susceptibility; rather, he uses that susceptibility to both eliminate and create motives.

The point about creation should be emphasized. Until now, we have focused on the elimination of motives, but the above example illustrates how thinking and reasoning can create, as well as eliminate, motives. As I remarked at the beginning, this capacity to eliminate and create motives through thinking and reasoning gives us a certain mastery over our susceptibilities to motivation. Through this capacity, we can employ reason to shape our lives instead of having our lives dominated by motives that lie outside reason's dominion. Such mastery figures prominently in the accounts of freedom and personhood.

Additional Points

There are two additional points about motives that we will need in the following chapters.

1. It will be important in the next chapter that a motive provides a justification for action—subject to two qualifications. First, the justification a motive provides is only some degree of justification. For a motive to provide a justification to do A does not require that the motive make doing A better justified than anything else one might do; it requires only that the motive provide some degree of justification for doing A.

The second—and more important—qualification is that a motive's justificatory power is defeasible. This defeasible character of the justification provided by motives is reflected in the fact that we often speak of, for example, envy, anger, and fear in explaining behavior without committing ourselves in any way on the question of whether or not those motives justify the behavior. Thus a motive provides a justification, other things being equal. But in the case of motives such as envy, anger, and fear, other things are often not equal.

These remarks may seem obviously wrong: it may seem obvious that a motive's justificatory power is not defeasible. After all, isn't "Doing A satisfies a desire" always at least some justification for doing A? To see that the answer is no, consider this case. Jones has a sudden desire—a yen—to drink a can of yellow paint. He realizes that he has a variety of important desires—for example, the desire for continued health, the desire not to upset his wife—the satisfaction of which would be significantly impaired if he were to drink the paint, and he regards his yen to drink the paint as a bizarre urge that will soon pass and one that he would greatly regret satisfying. Satisfying the desire to drink the paint would be distinctly unpleasant, as Jones knows; moreover, we may suppose that scarcely any effort is required to resist acting on the desire and that resisting acting on the desire does not give rise to any experience of frustration or dissatisfaction. Indeed, we may even suppose that

Jones enjoys having and resisting the yen. The spectacle of himself with such a bizarre desire amuses him.

In such a case, there is simply no justification—however, mini-mal—that the yen provides for drinking the paint. Consider an analogy with the relation between justification and belief. Suppose we know that Miller intends to deceive Dixon into thinking that he (Miller) will repay Smith. We overhear Miller promise Dixon that he will repay Smith. Given what we know, Miller's promise provides no justification for the belief that he will repay Smith. Similarly, given the totality of Jones's desires, the yen does not provide *any* degree of justification for drinking the paint. To think that it does is to overlook the fact—obvious in the repayment ex-ample—that the context can be such that a consideration that nor-mally provides a justification does do so in that context.

If other things were equal, that desire would be a justification for Jones's drinking the paint—if, for example, Jones drank a concoc-tion that coated his entire digestive tract so that the paint could have no ill effects (and would also taste like lemonade). So even in the original example, the yen counts as a motive since all that is required is that it would—if other things were equal—be a justification.

2. The second paint is terminological and trivial. When I intro-duced the expression 'structured motives', I did not explicitly note (because it was not relevant) that such motives can legitimately be described as desires—call them 'structured desires'. They can be so described since any motive is a desire (either an E-desire or an S-desire[24]). The reason for making this point explicit is simply that it proves convenient to use 'desire' terminology to describe struc-tured motives when drawing the connections between freedom and happiness.

Now let us turn to freedom.

---

24. Whether a structured desire is an E-desire or an S-desire depends on whether the component motive is an E-desire or an S-desire.

2 Freedom

Kant distinguishes two sorts of motives in his treatment of freedom: those supplied by reason in its practical employment, and those originating in our animal nature. Motives of the first sort—call them 'preferred motives'—are judgments: specifically, judgments that an action is in accord with the Categorical Imperative.[1] Examples of motives of the second sort are hunger, thirst, and sexual desire. To have the ability to act freely is to have the ability to act on preferred motives, even in face of opposition from nonpreferred motives. Let us call an account of freedom 'Kantian' provided that it has the same structure as Kant's analysis: provided that it distinguishes between preferred and nonpreferred motives and identifies the ability to act freely with the ability to act on the preferred motives even in the face of opposition from the nonpreferred. To qualify as Kantian an account may, but need not, identify the preferred motives with judgments; it may, but need not, identify the nonpreferred motives with desires that have their source in our animal nature.

This chapter develops a Kantian analysis of freedom where (certain) E-desires are the preferred motives, and S-desires are prominent (but not the only) examples of nonpreferred motives. In

---

1. Immanuel Kant, *Foundations of the Metaphysics of Morals*, trans. Lewis White Beck (Indianapolis: Bobbs-Merrill, 1959), p. 65f.

offering an analysis of the ability to act freely, I am (in the case of freedom) taking the notion of the ability to be prior to the notion of the act; that is, I will explain acting freely in terms of possession and use of the ability to act freely.

Freedom and Ability

My starting point is the observation that there are clear cases in which a limitation of a person's ability to act on his desires is a limitation of his freedom. The limitation may be external: one is tied up; or it may be internal: one is so afraid of sharks that any attempt to swim in the ocean ends in an uncontrollable dash away from the water. As the examples suggest, by 'ability' I mean the ability to act at a specific time. The necessary and sufficient condition of having an ability at a time is that one would succeed in acting at that time if one were to try. For example, Edwards ordinarily lifts three hundred pounds with ease. But at this moment, she tries but fails and therefore lacks the ability at the specific time.[2] Having noted the dependence of the ability on time, I will from

---

2. It is the notion of ability at a time that is essential to understanding free action; see Stuart Hampshire, *Freedom of the Individual*, expanded ed. (Princeton, N.J.: Princeton University Press, 1975), chap. 1. One might think that problems arise from the counterfactual nature of the notion of having an ability at a specific time: the necessary and sufficient condition of having an ability at a time is that one would succeed in acting at that time if one were to try. Like all counterfactuals, the truth or falsity of this counterfactual is a function of background assumptions. See David Lewis, *Counterfactuals* (Cambridge: Harvard University Press, 1973), chap. 1. This may seem to render the answer to "Do you have the ability to act freely?" indeterminate. Thus suppose that you are asleep. Do you have the ability to act freely? That is, would you so act if you tried? Of course, you cannot try unless you first wake up, but in asking what would happen if you were to try, we are asking what would happen if—in conditions under which you could try—you did try. We want to know what would happen if you were awake. Surely, if you were awake, you would succeed in acting if you tried. Or would you? You would not if, were you to awaken, an assassin would kill you instantly at the exact moment of your trying to do anything. You would not if you were to try to move your right leg because any attempt to do so would cause a severe cramp in that leg. And so on. Whether you succeed in acting depends on the background conditions we imagine you acting under. So isn't the answer indeterminate—varying as we vary our background assumptions? No. The answer does vary as we vary background assumptions, but we cannot—rationally—vary background assumptions at will. Choice of background assumptions is a principled, nonarbitrary matter. This makes the answer determinate.

now on routinely suppress reference to time when talking of the ability to act freely.

I take it for granted that having the ability to act on one's desires is a necessary condition of having the ability to act freely. Or that is almost right. One need not have the ability to act on every desire one has. One may want to raise one's paralyzed arm, but even without the ability to act on that desire one still has the ability to act freely. What is required is that one have the ability to act on a *suitable range* of one's desires. Perhaps the possession of the ability to act freely is a matter of degree: the more of one's desires on which one has the ability to act, the greater one's degree of freedom.[3] There is no need to settle this issue here, nor is there any need to say what counts as a suitable range. There is also no need to settle questions about the sense of 'ability'. There are familiar puzzles about freedom and determinism here. Should we think of one's having the ability as determined by various causal factors? We might think of possession of the ability on the model of the possession of a dispositional property: to have the ability to act on one's desires is to be disposed to do so in appropriate circumstances. Possession of the disposition would be seen as the result of a variety of heterogeneous causal factors. Or should we hold that freedom is incompatible with such causal determination? Nothing I will say requires taking a position on these issues.

Even though we are putting to one side questions about the sense of 'ability', one might still complain of a certain artificiality in my talk of exercising the ability to act freely. Not that the idea of exercising the ability somehow fails to make sense; if one has an ability, it makes good sense to talk about the exercise of that ability. However, wouldn't it be more natural, in the context of talk about freedom, to talk instead about willing or forming and acting on intentions? Perhaps; both willing and intending are certainly intimately tied to the exercise of the ability to act freely. However, there are a variety of ways one might fit talk of willing (if one wants to engage in such talk at all) on to the account of freedom that I

---

3. Compare Gary Watson, "Free Agency," in Gary Watson, ed., *Free Will* (New York: Oxford University Press, 1982), p. 96: "According to one familiar conception of freedom a person is free *to the extent that* he is able to do or get what he wants" (my italics). Let me add here that, while my focus in what follows will be on bodily actions, I do not mean to exclude mental actions, such as trying to remember.

will offer, and there is no need to pick one of these ways here. The same holds for talk of forming and acting on intentions. So I think it is actually clearer, in the long run, simply to talk noncommittally of exercising the ability to act freely.

The question to focus on is whether possession of the ability to act on a suitable range of one's desires is necessary and sufficient for having the ability to act freely. The idea that it is sufficient as well as necessary is attractive in its simplicity. But as Gary Watson points out in his excellent article "Free Agency," the objection is:

> Frequently enough, we say, or are inclined to say, that a person is not in control of his own actions, that he is not a 'free agent' with respect to them, even though his behavior is intentional. Possible examples of this sort of action include those that are explained by addictions, manias, and phobias of various sorts. But the concept of free action would seem to be pleonastic on the analysis of freedom in terms of the ability to get what one wants. For if a person does something intentionally, then surely he was able at that time to do it. Hence, on this analysis, he was free to do it. . . . Accordingly, this account would seem to embody a conflation of free action and intentional action.[4]

Watson has the following sort of case in mind. Edwards and Jones are riding in an elevator; Edwards intends to get off at the eleventh floor; Jones, at the twentieth. Jones, who suffers from a phobia about being in elevators, got into the elevator thinking that he could control his phobia, but at the eleventh floor, when Edwards walks out, Jones bolts after her. Although overpowered by his phobia, Jones leaves the elevator intentionally: getting out is what he intends to do. So given the connection between acting intentionally and being able to act, we must agree that Jones is *able* to perform the action of leaving the elevator. Moreover, it would seem that he has the ability to act on a suitable range of his desires: for example, suppose that when he bolts out of the elevator, he is acting not just on his desire to get out of the elevator but also on his desire to get to the twentieth floor. He thinks, "I'll use the stairs"; while he bolts from the elevator, he does so in as orderly a way as possible, acting on his desire to conceal from Edwards the fact that he has been overcome by

4. Watson, "Free Agency," pp. 96–97.

his phobia and so forth. Nonetheless, Jones, unlike Edwards, does not exit the elevator freely. On the contrary, he cannot help himself.

Watson takes examples of this sort to motivate a Kantian account of freedom. He is right; but to see why, we first need to note a fundamentally important connection between freedom and justification.

Freedom and Justification

I begin with an example. Mason is on the way to a political fundraising dinner at which he is the speaker. As he drives along, he daydreams about telling the audience what he really thinks of them: that they are hypocritical pseudoliberals with no genuine social conscience. However, although he desires to denounce the audience, he does not take the desire to provide any justification for action. He realizes that, in addition to having considerations about his obligations to others, he has a whole range of desires, the satisfaction of which would be greatly hindered by denouncing his audience.[5] But when he stands up to talk and looks at the audience, he can (because he has drunk too much) only see them as hypocritical pseudoliberals; to his horror, he hears himself denounce them as such. He tries to stop but cannot.

Helplessly in the grip of his desire to denounce, Mason is not acting freely. But this is not to say that he lacks the ability to act on suitable range of his desires. In addition to denouncing the audience, he could light a cigarette, take a drink of water, jump off the stage into the audience for dramatic effect, and so on. Lack of the ability to act on his desires is not what makes Mason count as acting unfreely: it is the lack of the ability to act on the desire that he takes to provide a *justification* for action. More exactly, it is the lack of the ability to do so *even in the face of opposing desires (like the desire to denounce) that do not provide justifications*. Freedom involves an element of self-mastery: we require of a free agent that he be the master of his own desires, able to overcome opposition from those desires.

It is worth emphasizing that self-mastery requires the ability to

---

5. In saying that Mason thinks there is no justification, I mean to exclude even the possibility that he unconsciously thinks there is.

act on desires that one takes to provide justifications, not on desires that actually do provide justifications. Suppose that Mason is simply mistaken when he thinks that the desire to give the speech provides no justification for doing so. He fails to realize that giving the speech will simply perpetuate his present unhappy way of life while denouncing the audience would harm no one and would be the act that would propel him out of his present life into a much happier one. This does not change the fact that Mason acts unfreely when he denounces the audience; he lacks self-mastery because he cannot act on the desire that he takes—wrongly—to provide a justification.

These considerations suggest a Kantian account of freedom in which the preferred motives are identified with desires that one takes to provide justifications for action; and the nonpreferred motives, with desires that one does not take to provide justifications. Note that it is here that it begins to be important that a desire is not always a justification for action. If a desire were always a justification for action, we could not build the account of the ability to act freely around the distinction between desires that do and those that do not provide justifications.

Now let us return to the elevator example. We should distinguish two versions. In the first, Jones takes his desire to ride to the twentieth floor to provide a justification for doing so but does *not* take his phobia-generated desire to provide any justification for leaving the elevator. Thus when Jones bolts from the elevator, he is overpowered by a desire that he does not take to provide a justification for action; overpowered in this way, Jones does not count as acting freely. His plight is exactly analogous to Mason's in the political-speech example; Mason is also overpowered by a desire that he does not take to provide a justification. In the second version of the example, Jones does take the phobia-generated desire to leave the elevator to provide a justification. He thinks, "There is a good reason to get out if I am this frightened." Nonetheless, he still acts unfreely when he bolts from the elevator. The reason is that in the grip of his phobia, he could not have done otherwise; although he can and does act on his desire to leave, it is also true that he cannot help but act on that desire. The fact that he regards the desire to leave as a justification for action is, as it were, a sheer accident. He would have acted on that desire even if he had not regarded it as providing a justification. His so acting is not evidence of self-mastery but of the lack of it; hence he should be regarded as acting unfreely.

The suggested Kantian analysis of freedom accommodates this case quite easily, but we need to state the account somewhat more carefully. Let R be a suitable range of one's desires, where one takes each desire in R to provide a justification for action. Then:

(1) one has the ability to act freely if and only if one has the ability to act on each desire in R, even when so acting is contrary to one or more of the desires that one does not take to provide justifications.

The point is that if one has the ability to act on each desire in R, then, no matter what one in fact does, one *could have* acted on any desire in the range. This secures that "I could have done otherwise" is something that is true if one acts when one has the ability to act freely. Two further points are in order.

First, the qualification "even when so acting is contrary to one or more of the desires that one does not take to provide justifications" is, strictly speaking, unnecessary. If one has the ability, at a certain time, to act on each desire in R, it follows that one has the ability to do so even in the face of opposition from desires that one does not take to be justifications for action. Still, it is worth including the qualification in the analysis to emphasize the important point that freedom involves an element of self-mastery, that to have the ability to act freely is to be the master of one's own desires. Second, the concept of taking needs a brief gloss. To take a desire to provide a justification is to be such that one would, in appropriate circumstances, sincerely produce the desire as a justification. Taking so conceived need not be something the taker is explicitly aware of; taking may be unconscious. Indeed, even if asked for one's justification, one might not, because of self-deception, lack of self-knowledge, or whatever, cite the relevant desire(s), although one would if disclosures were unhampered by self-deception, lack of self-knowledge, and the like. We frequently take our desires to be justifications; we are frequently prepared to cite our desires in (sincere) answer, or in partial answer, to the question "Why did you do it?"—the question being understood as requesting a justification.

So far, I have argued for (1) by appealing to examples. However, there is another good reason to accept (1); it explains—or, more accurately, partially explains—a fundamental intuition about freedom. Aristotle expresses the intuition this way: one acts freely when "the starting point of the motion of parts of the body ... is in one-self."[6] Kant expresses the same idea when he defines freedom as that property of the will "by which it can be effective independently of foreign causes determining it."[7] 'Foreign causes' are causes that lie "outside" the agent. Any adequate definition of freedom must incorporate and elucidate this fundamental intuition. But it is not a simple matter to do so. All we have is the metaphor of a boundary around agents—outside the boundary causes are "foreign"; inside, they are not. It is a major consideration in favor of (1) that it con-tributes to making literal sense of the "foreign causes" metaphor.

Consider that the person who satisfies (1) has, with respect to a range R desires, the ability to act on each desire in R. To exercise this ability is to ensure that one acts on this desire instead of any other desire: that is, one imposes on oneself a certain cause of action. The fact that the cause is self-imposed partially explicates the sense in which the cause is not "foreign"—the idea being that what is *self*-imposed is not "foreign" or "outside" the agent.[8] When one is overpowered by desires, the cause of the action is "foreign" or "outside" in the sense that it makes one act contrary to what one would do if one were able to impose a cause of action on oneself. There is a further point to note: according to (1), the desires in R are desires that one *takes to provide justifications for action*. This is essential to the explication of "in"-ness in terms of self-imposed causes, for a self-imposed cause is "nonforeign" only if the cause is a desire one takes to be justification for action. A variant of the political speech example shows why. Imagine that Mason, as he drives along, has two daydreams. He daydreams about denouncing the audience, and he also daydreams about walking to the podium,

---

6. *Nicomachean Ethics*, trans. Martin Ostwald (Indianapolis: Bobbs-Merrill, 1962), 1110a16.

7. Kant, *Foundations of the Metaphysics of Morals*, p. 65f.

8. There is a close connection here with the Kantian identification of freedom with self-legislation; a self-legislating being imposes causes on itself, and this is part of the reason Kant regards such a being as free.

making an obscene gesture, and walking out. He wants to denounce and wants to make the gesture, but he does not take either desire to be a justification for action. Nonetheless, when he stands up to give the speech, he begins to denounce the audience; he tries to stop, but he cannot. That is, he cannot stop *and* begin to give his prepared speech. He could stop, give the obscene gesture, and walk away. So he has the ability to impose a cause of action on himself: he can act on the desire to give the gesture instead of the desire to denounce. But if he were to exercise this ability, he would still not be acting freely. For free action, the self-imposed cause must be one that one takes to provide a justification for action.

It is worth noting that, given this explication of "in"-ness, we can subsume the idea that freedom involves self-mastery under the idea that in free action the source of the action is "in" the agent. Self-mastery (as we noted earlier) consists in being able to overcome opposition from one's own desires so that one can act on those desires one takes to provide justifications. One is able to do exactly that if one has the ability to impose a cause of action on oneself, where the cause is a desire one takes to be a justification for action.

These remarks provide only a partial explication of the sense in which the source of free action is "in" the agent, for as we will see later, the explication in terms of self-imposed causes omits four other important aspects of "in"-ness. Nonetheless, this partial explication constitutes a strong case for the account given in (1). With essential additions, I will argue that the definition is indeed correct. But first it is worth comparing (1) with two other contemporary Kantian analyses of freedom: one, Harry Frankfurt's; the other, Gary Watson's. The comparison clarifies the role of the concept of justification in (1).

Frankfurt's account.[9]   Frankfurt offers an account of freedom of the *will*, and to have freedom of the will in his sense is not to have what I am calling 'the ability to act freely'. Nonetheless, if we combine what Frankfurt says about freedom of the will with what he says about freedom to act, the result is a Kantian analysis of the ability to act freely. The preferred motives on this account are those

9. The position I have in mind is in Harry G. Frankfurt, "Freedom of the Will and the Concept of a Person," in Watson, *Free Will.*

toward which one does have, or would have in appropriate circumstances, a certain attitude: one does or would desire that the motive be effective—that it actually cause action. To have the ability to act freely is to have the ability to act on such motives even in the face of opposition from motives that one does not desire to be effective.[10] Thus in Frankfurt's account, the appeal to second-order desires in effect replaces the appeal in (1) to the attitude of taking-to-justify.

This means that Frankfurt's analysis is quite different from the analysis in (1), for taking a desire to provide a justification neither entails nor is entailed by desiring that a motive be effective. To see this, consider a variant of the political-speech example. When Mason stands up to talk and looks out on the audience, he sees them as hypocritical pseudoliberals; filled with the desire to denounce, he also finds himself—in the midst of his sudden intense loathing of the audience—desiring that that desire be effective. Still, Mason does not take the desire to denounce to provide a justification for action. To see a desire as providing a justification for action is to see it as weighing—in a nonarbitrary and principled way—in favor of that action; Mason's attitude toward the desire to denounce is that it does not weigh at all in favor of denouncing the audience. So, desiring that a motive be effective does not entail taking that desire to provide a justification. Nor does taking a desire to provide a justification entail desiring that the desire be effective. Mason does take his desire to give the speech to be a justification for doing so; however, when Mason, filled with intense loathing, looks out

10. To understand that Frankfurt holds this position, consider these two passages. (1) "When we ask whether a person's will is free we are not asking whether he is in a position to translate his first-order desires into action. That is the question of whether he is free to do as he pleases" (ibid., p. 90). (2) "It seems to me both natural and useful to construe the question of whether a person's will is free in close analogy to the question of whether an agent enjoys freedom of action. Now freedom of action is (roughly, at least) the freedom to do what one wants to do. Analogously, then, the statement that a person enjoys freedom of will means (also roughly) that he is free to will what he wants to will. More precisely, it means that he is free to will what he wants to will, or to have the will he wants" (ibid., p. 90). To have the ability to act freely is to be free "to will what [one] wants" and to be in "a position to translate one's first-order desires into action"—that is, certain of one's first-order desires, the one's one desires to be effective. So, on Frankfurt's view, to have the ability to act freely is to have the ability to act on desires that one desires to be effective.

on the audience, he has no desire that the desire to give the speech be effective; the desire that he desires to be effective is the desire to denounce. He is so carried away that his thought is "Justification be damned!" and he desires *not* to act on the desire that he takes to be a justification.

Some may think that it is better to avoid the concept of justification in the definition of freedom as Frankfurt does rather than build it in as (1) does. After all, this allows Frankfurt to give a simple and clear characterization of the class of preferred motives; they are just those motives with respect to which one has a certain second-order desire. If we follow (1) and characterize preferred motives in terms of justification, we face the question: what counts as justification? Why saddle ourselves with this question if we do not have to? But we do have to. To see why, imagine Mason berating the audience for being hypocritical pseudoliberals. Overpowered by his desire to denounce, Mason lacks the ability to act freely. Yet he has the ability to act on desires that he desires to be effective; indeed, he is doing so when he acts on his desire to denounce. So the ability to act on desires that one desires to be effective cannot be the same as the ability to act freely. Moreover, the reason Mason lacks the ability to act freely is that, overpowered by a desire that he does not take to provide a justification for action, he is unable to act on a desire that he does take to provide a justification. So it would seem that an appeal to the notion of justification must play some role in the definition of freedom.

In reply, one could argue that Frankfurt's account—or, more accurately, a revised version of that account—adequately explains why Mason acts unfreely. To see the revision, consider Frankfurt's discussion of decisive identification (in what follows, 'second order volition' is Frankfurt's technical term for a desire that a desire be effective):

> When a person identifies *decisively* with one of his first-order desires, this commitment 'resounds' throughout the potentially endless array of higher order desires. Consider a person who without reservation or conflict, wants to be motivated by the desire to concentrate on his work. The fact that his second-order volition to be moved by this desire is a decisive one means that there is no room for questions concerning the pertinence of desires or volitions of higher orders. Suppose the person is asked whether he wants to

want to want to concentrate on his work. He can properly insist that this question concerning a third-order desire does not arise. It would be a mistake to claim that, because he has not considered whether he wants the second-order volition he has formed, he is indifferent to the question of whether it is with this volition or with some other that he wants his will to accord. The decisiveness of the commitment he has made means that he has decided that no further question about his second-order volition, at any higher order, remains to be asked. It is relatively unimportant whether we explain this by saying that this commitment implicitly generates an endless series of confirming desires of higher orders, or by saying that the commitment is tantamount to a dissolution of the pointedness of all questions concerning higher orders of desire.[11]

One could argue that Frankfurt's analysis of freedom really is—or at least should be—the following: one has the ability to act freely if and only if one does (or would in appropriate circumstances) *decisively identify* with at least one desire, and one has the ability to act on desires with which one decisively identifies—even in the face of opposition from desires with which one does not so identify. Then one could argue that Mason fails to act freely because he does not "identify decisively" with either the desire to give the speech or with the desire to denounce. After all, it is surely not the case that Mason, "without reservation or conflict, wants to be motivated" by either of the two desires; there is "room for questions concerning the pertinence of desires or volitions of higher orders."

The problem with this reply is with the notion of decisive identification. What is it? It cannot be simply the having of appropriate higher-order desires. The reason is that the reply to the Mason example depends on the fact that one can have the relevant higher order desires without decisive identification. Indeed, Frankfurt himself explains decisive identification in terms of the concept of decision: "The decisiveness of the commitment he has made means that he has decided that no further question about his second-order volition, at any higher order, remains to be asked." Is this decision something for which the person has a justification? This is the natural way of understanding Frankfurt's talk of decision, for the natural idea is that one decisively identifies with a desire provided that one thinks there is a decisive case for acting on that desire.

11. Ibid., pp. 91–92.

But this would be to explain 'decision' in terms of justification, and the appeal to second-order desires would turn out to be a long detour back to the notion of justification.

But suppose we were to hold that the decision involved in decisive identification is not one the agent need see as backed by any justification. The problem is that this leaves the connection between decision and decisive identification completely unclear. Indeed, why isn't a second-order desire enough for "decision" in the relevant sense? Why isn't it the case that Mason identifies with his desire to denounce when, thinking "Justification be damned!", he desires that that desire be effective? I see no satisfactory way to answer this question that does not at some point bring in the notion of justification of action.

Watson's account. Watson begins his Kantian analysis of freedom by criticizing 'the familiar view of freedom', the view that freedom consists simply and entirely in the ability to act on one's desires. As we saw earlier, Watson criticizes this view for involving a "conflation of free action and intentional action." To avoid this conflation, Watson suggests that we draw

> a distinction between wanting and valuing which will enable the familiar view of freedom to make sense of the notion of an unfree action. The contention will be that, in the case of actions that are unfree, the agent is unable to get what he most wants, or *values*, and this inability is due to his own "motivational system." In this case the obstruction to the action that he most wants to do is his own will. It is in this sense that the agent is unfree: the agent is obstructed in and by the very performance of the action.[12]

The idea, as Watson goes on to explain, is that the ability to act freely is the ability to act in accord with what one values even in the face of opposition from one's desires.[13] On Watson's view, then, the preferred motives are *valuings*; the nonpreferred, *desires*.

Watson's talk of valuing conflates two things we have distinguished: a special kind of motivation and taking oneself to have a justification for action. To value is clearly to have a motive; indeed, Watson says that "in part, to value something is, in the appropriate

12. Watson, "Free Agency," p. 97.
13. See ibid., pp. 105f.

circumstances, to want it."[14] And, to value is, at least typically, to take oneself to have a justification for action, for as Watson explains, "We might say that an agent's values consist in those principles and ends which he—in a cool and non-self-deceptive moment—articulates as definitive of the good, fulfilling, and defensible life."[15] Watson tries to explain what is special about valuings as motives—what distinguishes valuing from desiring—by appealing to the link with the good: "the notion of value is tied to (cannot be understood independently of) those of the good and worthy, it is one thing to value (think good) a state of affairs and another to desire that it obtain. However, to think a thing good is at the same time to desire it (or its promotion)."[16]

The problem is that this is not an adequate explanation of the distinction between valuing and desiring. It is essential to Watson's position that "to think a thing good is at the same time to desire it," for it is essential that to value is to have a certain kind of motive. This is why Watson insists that to value is—in some sense—to desire. But it is unclear in what sense; what does 'desire' mean in the phrase "to think a thing good is at the same time to desire it"? Does it mean desire in the sense of 'desire' in which to desire is *not* to value? This cannot be right; to value would then be to desire in the very sense of 'desire' in which that word is supposed to pick out a kind of motive that is not an instance of valuing. There is another possibility. At one point, Watson explains that he is "going to use 'want' and 'desire' in the very inclusive sense now familiar in philosophy, whereby virtually any motivational factor that may figure in the explanation of intentional action is a want."[17] To value is certainly to desire in this sense. The problem is that both valuings and desirings (in the sense opposed to valuing) are desires in this sense. So we still need an explanation of 'value' and 'desire' on which each word picks out a kind of motive that is not the kind of motive picked out by the other. I do not see how such an explanation can be given by appeal to the notion of the good.

I think Watson is mistaken in trying to appeal to the good to define valuings as a special subclass of motives; indeed, I think that

14. Ibid., p. 105.
15. Ibid.
16. Ibid., p. 99.
17. Ibid., p. 98 n.2.

he is wrong in holding that the notion of the good enters into the definition of freedom at all. The notion of taking-to-justify plays a role in the account, but to take a desire to provide a justification for action is not the same as having an end that one "would—in a cool and non-self-deceptive moment—[articulate] as definitive of the good, fulfilling, and defensible life." One reason for the difference is that what one, in the heat of the moment, takes to be a justification need not coincide with what one would coolly and nonself-deceptively regard "as definitive of the good, fulfilling, and defensible life."

Despite this difference, I am in agreement with Watson on one essential point: a special kind of motive is involved in having the ability to act freely. But these special motives are not Watson's valuings; indeed, my strategy is just the reverse of his. Whereas he explains freedom in terms of valuing, I will—in Chapter 5—*use the definition of the ability to act freely to explain valuing*. This explanation rests in part on the fact that freedom involves a special kind of motive.

To see that freedom does involve such a motive, let us return to (1) and consider two counterexamples. Each one points to a different defect, and each defect can be remedied by recognizing that a special kind of motive is involved in free action. For the first counterexample, imagine a creature that satisfies (1): it has the ability to act on each desire in a certain suitable range, where it takes each desire in that range to provide a justification for action. But everything that it desires has been entirely predetermined by us—the ones who created it. We "programmed" the creature to desire only certain things. For example, since it has to hunt for food in an environment in which food is scarce, and in which purple berries are poisonous, we built in a desire to hunt for food, and we designed the creature so that it never wants to eat purple berries.

The creature does not have the ability to act freely, for—I contend—to have the ability to act freely is, in part, to have the ability, through thinking and reasoning, to eliminate and create motives. The creature lacks the ability to act freely since we designed it with a fixed, unmodifiable set of motives. The underlying intuition here is the one mentioned earlier: in free action the cause of the action is "in" the agent, not "foreign." As we saw earlier, (1) yields a partial explication in terms of self-imposed causes: a person who satisfies (1) has, with respect to a suitable range R of desires that the person takes to provide justifications, the ability to act on each desire in R; to exercise this ability is to impose on oneself a certain cause of action—to ensure that one acts on this desire instead of any other. Now suppose in addition that the person can eliminate and create motives; then it is up to him (in part, at least) what desires are in the range R. Having the ability to create and eliminate motives, he can add to and subtract from this range. This means that there is a double sense in which motives can be self-imposed: one can impose on oneself a motive from the range R, and one can, by adding to and subtracting from R, impose on oneself the range of motives available for self-imposition in the first sense.

But why think that having the ability to act freely involves this double self-imposition of motives? The idea has intuitive appeal; indeed, it is part of a long philosophical tradition about freedom. Plato and Kant, for example, both see freedom as involving the rational determination of motivation.[18] But we can do more than appeal to intuition here, for the concept of freedom does not stand on its own. It is part of a network of concepts—a network that plays a fundamental descriptive and explanatory role for us.[19] Concepts in this network include personhood, enjoyment, and happiness. One function of the concept of freedom in this network is to mark the distinction between beings that are, and those that are not, able to eliminate and create motives through thinking and reasoning; indeed, the fact that freedom marks this distinction turns out to be

18. The failure to mention Aristotle here in the same breath with Plato and Kant is not inadvertent. Aristotle holds that animals have a share in voluntary action because the source of their movements is "in" them, but it is not clear that he thinks that insofar as animals share in voluntary action, they must not be slaves to the present moment. In Aristotle, it is the capacity for choice that makes one free of the tyranny of the present (see the *Nicomachean Ethics*, 1111b6 f.).

19. Sidgwick (echoing Kant) notes the importance of the concept of freedom in our thought about ourselves: "I can suppose that my conviction of free choice *may* be illusory: that if I knew my own nature I *might* see to be predetermined that... I should act... contrary to my rational judgment. But I cannot conceive of myself seeing this, without at the same time conceiving of my whole conception of what I now call 'my' action fundamentally altered: I cannot conceive that if I contemplated the actions of my organism in this light I should refer them to my 'self'—i.e. to the mind so contemplating them—in the sense in which I now refer to them." Henry Sidgwick, *The Methods of Ethics*, 7th ed. (Indianapolis: Hackett, 1981), pp. 65–66.

essential in drawing the connections between freedom and person-hood. The way to establish this claim is to exhibit in a convincing way the conceptual interconnections between freedom, person-hood, enjoyment, and happiness, and I will do so in the chapters that follow. For now, I am assuming that having the ability to act freely requires that one be able through thinking and reasoning to eliminate and create motives.

We can incorporate this requirement into the account of freedom by identifying the preferred motives with conceptions serving as E-desires (that one takes to provide a justification for action). Con-ceptions that serve as E-desires are—in the sense explained in Chap-ter 1—intrinsically responsive to reasoning. As we noted in Chapter 1, it is an essential feature of reasoning that it can alter our con-ceptions of things: thoughts are (paramount among) the inputs and outputs of the mental process that is reasoning, and reasoning is necessarily a process that has the power to alter our thoughts. So conceptions—as complexes of thoughts—are intrinsically the sort of thing that reasoning can alter (by showing them to be false, incomplete, unrealistic, or in some other way faulty). This makes the E-desires provided by our conceptions intrinsically responsive to reason, for when reason eliminates the conception that provides the desire, it thereby eliminates the desire—the desire being the conception. It will prove convenient to refer to such desires simply as 'E-desires' from now on, instead of 'conceptions serving as E-desires'; this shorthand should cause no confusion, even though strictly speaking, it does not follow from the fact that something is an E-desire that it is a conception serving as such a desire, an E-desire is *any* state-token serving as a motive, where not every token of that state is a motive. Conceptions are, however, the only ex-amples of such state-tokens that I know of and the only examples with which we are concerned here.

There is an objection to consider. One might think that it is a mistake to identify the preferred motives with E-desires since this means that only E-desires qualify as preferred motives. This may seem wrong. After all, one can take an S-desire to be a justification for action, and the leading idea of the account of freedom is that the ability to act freely is the ability to act on desire one takes to be justifications. So why shouldn't one count as lacking the ability to act freely if one is unable to act on a suitable range of S-desires?

This objection confuses a limitation on one's ability to act freely with the complete lack of the ability. Let us grant—what is undeniable—that the inability to act on an S-desire (which one takes to provide a justification) is certainly a restriction of one's freedom. For example, suppose one took one's S-desire to eat ice cream as a justification for doing so but was so overwhelmed by fear of gaining weight that one was unable to do anything but throw the dish of ice cream against the wall in sheer panic at the thought of eating it. This inability is a restriction of one's freedom. In general, one is freer to the extent that one can act on S-desires (which one takes to provide justifications). But: it is enough to qualify as having the ability to act freely that one have the ability to act on a suitable range of one's E-desires. In support of this claim, consider that it is conceivable that a being should have only E-desires; it is, after all, a contingent fact about us that we are beings that have S-desires. Now a being that had only E-desires could still have the ability to act freely; so having S-desires cannot be a necessary condition of having the ability to act freely. However, having E-desires is a necessary condition: without such desires one lacks motives intrinsically responsive to reasoning.

For the second counterexample to (1), imagine a creature all of whose desires are for current sensory experiences. It never desires an experience that is not presently occurring; when a desired experience ceases, the desire for it ceases as well. Its desires come and go as its sensory experiences come and go; this is not to say that it desires every sensory experience it has but that whatever it does desire is an ongoing sensory experience. It takes some of these desires to be justifications for action. For example, if it is eating chocolate and desiring the experience of the taste, it may take this desire to provide a justification for having the experience. It has the ability to act on desires that it takes to be justifications for action, even in the face of opposition from desires that it does not take to provide justifications.

The creature satisfies (1), but it does not have the ability to act freely; for the creature is a slave to the present moment, and freedom consists in part in freedom from the tyranny of the present. To see what this claim amounts to, compare the creature to one of us. Imagine that when the alarm goes off early Saturday morning, you are sleepy and strongly desire to stay in bed. Nonetheless, you make yourself get out of bed. The explanation is that you want to go sailing frequently, and you planned on Friday to go sailing early Saturday morning. Despite the strength of your desire to stay in bed, you are able to act according to your plan. You are not a slave to the present moment. In general, to be free from the tyranny of the present is meet two conditions: first, one has desires to attain goals whose achievement requires a certain pattern of activity *over time* (the desire to sail *frequently* is a desire of this sort); second, one is able to act on these desires even in the face of opposition from desires for present experiences.

But why think that to have the ability to act freely, one must not be a slave to the present moment? It is tempting simply to appeal to intuition. Isn't is clear that not being a slave to the present is a necessary condition of having the ability to act freely? It has seemed so to others—Plato and Kant among them.[20] The underlying intuition here is again that, in the case of free action, the source of the action is "in" the agent. The idea is that this would not be true if the motives available to an agent were dictated by whatever that agent's present experience happened to be. A free being's motives are not dictated to it by "outside," "foreign" vagaries of present experience; its motives are, in part at least, dictated to it by itself independently of whatever its present experience happens to be.

We can do more than appeal to intuition here. As we noted earlier, the concept of freedom is part of a network of concepts. Personhood is one of the concepts in this network, and the fact that freedom involves not being a slave to the present turns out to be essential in delineating the connections between freedom and personhood, for (I will argue) a necessary condition of being a person is that one use one's ability to act freely to impose a certain order over time on one's thought and action. This fact about persons is, in turn, part of the foundation of the definition of leading a happy life. The systematic, informative character of these conceptual interconnections provides a good reason to think that not being a slave to the present is an aspect of freedom.

Let us assume then that freedom from the tyranny of the present is a necessary condition of having the ability to act freely, which

20. Again, for the reasons given in note 8, the failure to mention Aristotle is not inadvertent.

means, in part, that one who has the ability must have desires to attain goals whose achievement requires a certain pattern of activity over time. We can incorporate this requirement into the analysis of freedom by requiring that the E-desires involved in free action have a certain special content. Explaining the special content of the E-desires involved in freedom is the first step in revising (1).

Self-concepts

The E-desires in question are desires to realize *self-concepts* and not just any self-concepts but those of a special sort. A concept *c* is one of *x*'s concepts just in case *x* believes—consciously or unconsciously—that *c* applies to him. A self-concept, then, may be as intricate and detailed as a life plan or as simple as "I am raising my arm now." During one's life, one will form a vast number of self-concepts. One may think of oneself as a lawyer, sports fan, novel reader, and chess player; as drinking a cup of coffee now and as intending to go to the store; as a possible success, as a possible failure, as too reserved, and so on. The special self-concepts involved in free action are those realizable over time in a temporally extended series of experiences and activities. Examples are concepts such as *solving a crossword puzzle* or *being a sympathetic person*. To count as solving a crossword puzzle, a temporally extended series of one's experiences and activities must occur; and although it may be conceivable that one should count as a sympathetic person without manifesting the relevant experiences and activities, that concept may be, and typically is, realized in a temporally extended series of instances of feeling, expressing, and acting out of sympathy. Let us call such self-concepts 'expansive self-concepts.'

We need a fuller account of what an expansive self-concept is. There are two sorts of expansive self-concepts to distinguish: those that apply *both* to experiences and activities *and* to persons and those that apply to persons but not to experiences and activities. The concept *solving a crossword puzzle* illustrates the first case. When I work on a crossword puzzle, the concept *solving a crossword puzzle* applies to me; it also applies to my activity—the combination of writing, consulting the dictionary, trying to remember, and so on that I engage in when I try to solve the puzzle. That activity is the solving of the puzzle. Now—to introduce a point that turns out to be essential—suppose I work on the puzzle on and off throughout the day so that my solving of the crossword puzzle consists of temporally discontinuous stretches of activity. The concept applies to the totality of these separate stretches and also to each separate stretch in the totality.

By way of contrast, consider concepts like *raising one's arm* or *hitting a golf ball*. With one qualification, it is correct to say that neither of these concepts can be realized by a series of temporally discontinuous activities. The qualification is that one can—in a sense—raise one's arm or hit a golf ball in a series of temporally discontinuous activities. One can raise one's arm in a series of jerky movements, and the activity of hitting a golf ball is, in fact, often composed of two temporally discontinuous segments since it is common (and good form) to pause briefly at the top of the backswing. But in both cases, if temporal distance between the segments is too great, the segments taken as a whole will not count as a single unstructured instance of raising one's arm or of hitting a golf ball. In the case of solving a crossword puzzle, on the other hand, the members of the series may be quite temporally distant from one another.

There is a marked difference of degree here, and the point to stress is that expansive self-concepts are more like *solving a crossword puzzle* than *raising one's arm* or *hitting a golf ball*. That is, I shall take expansiveness to be a matter of degree and shall use 'expansive' for the *solving of crossword puzzle* end of the spectrum. There are many concepts at this end, for example: *making a million dollars a year, drinking ten cups of coffee a day, studying Aristotle, writing a book,* and *learning Greek*. These concepts are realizable over time in a temporally extended series of experiences and activities, where members of the series may be quite temporally distant from one another.

The second sort of expansive self-concept applies to persons but not to experiences and activities. The concept *being a sympathetic person* illustrates this case. Suppose that Smith is a sympathetic person and that this trait manifests itself in a temporally extended series of experiences and activities. We cannot say, as we did for *solving a crossword puzzle*, that the concept *applies* to those experiences and activities; the concept applies to persons only. How-

ever, there is an important relation between the experiences and
activities through which Smith manifests sympathy and the concept
being a sympathetic person. The essential point is that—in the
normal course of things, at least—a sympathetic person will have
certain sorts of experiences and engage in certain sorts of activities;
he will experience and do things that count as feeling, expressing,
and acting out of sympathy. I am not suggesting that such experiences and activities are a necessary condition of being a sympathetic
person. It is (perhaps) possible that, in (very) exceptional circumstances, one might count as a sympathetic person even if one never
felt, expressed, or acted out of sympathy. What is true, however,
is that—in the normal course of things—one cannot count as a
sympathetic person in the absence of such experiences and activities. I will say that experiences and activities of this sort *realize*
the concept—experiences and activities of the sort one must have,
in the normal course of things, in order to count as a sympathetic
person.

There are many other examples of realization; consider the expansive self-concepts that pick out character traits: *being coura-
geous* and *being trustworthy*, for example. However, character traits
are not the only examples; recall the list of "empirical selves" that
James gives in the passage quoted in the Introduction. James would
like to be a "wit, a *bon vivant*, a lady killer, as well as a philosopher,
a philanthropist, statesman, warrior, and African explorer, as well
as a 'tone poet', and saint." These are also expansive self-concepts
that are realizable in the sense explained.

We now have two ways of talking about the relation between
self-concepts and experiences and activities. Some self-concepts—
for example, *solving a crossword puzzle*—apply to experiences and
activities; others, such as *being a sympathetic person*, are realized
by experiences and activities. It will prove convenient to collapse
these two ways of talking into one. An easy way to do this is simply
to extend the sense of 'realize'. Thus an experience or activity φ
realizes the self-concept c if and only if c applies to φ or φ is the
sort of experience or activity one must—in the normal course of
things—exhibit if one is to count as someone to whom c applies.

Now we can characterize the E-desires involved in acting freely.
They are E-desires to continue to realize expansive self-concepts.
Recall that an E-desire (as we are now using the term) is a motivating

conception. The motivating conceptions involved in free action are conceptions of what it would be like to realize this or that expansive self-concept. More exactly, it is—for reasons that will emerge below—a conception of what it would be like to *continue* to realize an expansive self-concept; it serves as a motive to continue to realize the self-concept. Such a "could continue" conception represents one as having already realized the self-concept and as continuing to do so in the future. There is a qualification: sometimes the E-desire is (as we will see later) simply a conception that one could realize a self-concept—not a conception that one could continue to realize it. Typically, however, the E-desires will be "could continue" conceptions.

We can now state a revised account of the ability to act freely. Let R be a suitable range of E-desires to continue to realize expansive self-concepts, where one takes each desire in R to provide a justification for realizing the self-concept. Then:

> (2) one has the ability to act freely if and only if one has the ability to act on each desire in R, even when so acting is contrary to one or more of the desires that one does not take to provide justifications.

(2) avoids the counterexamples to (1).

Freedom from the tyranny of the present. To be free from the tyranny of the present is to have desires to attain goals whose achievement requires a certain pattern of activity over time and to be able to act on those desires even in the face of opposition from desires for present experiences. To satisfy (2) is to meet these conditions. According to (2), the E-desires involved in free action are conceptions about continuing to realize expansive self-concepts. An expansive self-concept is realized through a temporally extended series of experiences and activities, so to conceive that one could continue to realize such a self-concept is to believe that one initiated an appropriate self-concept-realizing series in the past and to believe that one could extend the series into the future. To have the ability to act on such desires is to have the ability to connect one's past and future so as to continue to realize expansive self-concepts. Moreover, to satisfy (2) is to be able to connect one's past

and future in this way even in the face of opposition from desires
that one does not take to provide justifications. Some of these non-
justifying desires will (or could) on occasion be desires for present
experiences, so one who satisfies (2) has the ability to connect his
past and future so as to continue to realize self-concepts even in
the face of opposition from desires for present experiences.

Opposing desires for present experiences are—in human beings,
in any case—frequently S-desires (although they need not always
be S-desires). For example, one E-desires to continue to realize the
self-concept *drinking less*, but one has a strong S-desire to drink
the scotch with which one's host has refilled one's glass. Of course,
the account of the ability to act freely does not require that opposing
desires ever have to take the form of S-desires; indeed, a being that
lacks S-desires entirely could satisfy the conditions given in (2).
However, our biological nature is such that S-desires for present
experiences will arise in us in certain circumstances, for the capacity to have certain S-desires—like the desire to drink (when one
is thirsty) or the desire to eat (when one is hungry)—is a species-
wide trait. Of course, not all S-desires are shared species-wide (e.g.,
a sudden yen for yellow paint).

Eliminating and creating motives.   To satisfy (2) is to be able to
act on E-desires. E-desires can be eliminated and created by reasoning. We made this point in Chapter 1, but it is worth two more
examples, if only to put the flesh of detail on the skeleton of theory.

Consider an example of elimination. The sixty-year-old Smith
(under the influence of television commercials that suggest that one
must at all costs be youthful) begins contemplating having a lover
one-third his age. The idea seems absurd at first, but his imagination
keeps returning to and playing with the idea, and a conception—
a complex of thoughts about what it would be like to realize the
self-concept *having a young lover*—gradually emerges. Now, Smith,
who is plagued by his awareness of his advanced age, is by virtue
of this very awareness especially susceptible to motivation by conceptions that represent him as still essentially youthful; for this
reason, the conception begins to serve as an E-desire to realize the
self-concept *having a young lover*. Finally, Smith takes the desire
to provide a justification for action and, acting on it, has his hair
styled, buys new clothes, and begins to frequent singles bars.

But as time passes, he begins to think that he is being ridiculous. He finds himself thinking, frequently and with approval, of the following remarks that he once read (he finds the sentimentality of the prose appealing):

> ordinarily we cling to our past and remain stuck in the illusion of youthfulness. Being old is highly unpopular. Nobody seems to consider that not being able to grow old is just about as absurd as not being able to outgrow child's-size shoes. A still infantile man of thirty is surely to be deplored, but a youthful septuagenerian—isn't that delightful? And yet both are perverse, lacking in style, psychological monstrosities. A young man who does not fight and conquer has missed to best part of his youth, and an old man who does not know how to listen to the secrets of the brooks, as they tumble down from the peaks, makes no sense; he is a spiritual mummy who is nothing but a rigid relic of the past. He stands apart from life, mechanically repeating himself to the last triviality.[21]

Under the impact of this passage, Smith begins to reason and reflect about—as he puts it to himself—"what it would really be like" to have a young lover. He thinks about the fact that in all the time he has spent recently in singles bars, he has talked to only one young woman, and that conversation he did not enjoy. His typical behavior is to find a quiet spot in the bar and drink alone in silence. It becomes clear to him that he has been avoiding even the remotest possibility of involvement with a young woman, and he sees that, unless very deeply ingrained attitudes change, having a young lover would, at best, be tedious and boring and, at worst, the abandonment of a way of life to which he is deeply attached. In reaching this conclusion, he has abandoned his previous conception of what it would be like to have a young lover; since that conception was his motive, he ceases to be motivated. This example is a fuller illustration of a point we emphasized in the last chapter: that the ability to eliminate and create motives through thinking and reasoning provides one with a certain mastery over one's susceptibilities to motivation. Such mastery is an essential element of the ability to act freely. The Smith example illustrates elimination; the following example, creation.

21. Carl Jung, "The Soul and Death," in *Structure and Dynamics of the Psyche* (Princeton, N.J.: Princeton University Press, 1969), p. 407.

Jones admires Schweitzer for devoting himself to the medical care of African tribesmen; he takes this to be a particularly praiseworthy example of respect for life, and he wishes he were motivated to do something similar, but he just isn't. However, Jones knows that he is susceptible to motivation by conceptions that vividly represent the suffering of others and that represent him as effectively putting an end to that suffering. With this in mind, Jones reads widely about the plight of the Third World, about the horrible suffering of starvation, about the disproportionate amount of the world's resources consumed by the United States, and so on; as he reads, he deliberately builds, through thinking and reasoning, a conception of what it is like to starve and of what he could do to help. The result is that this conception begins to serve as an unstructured motive. Thinking about the plight of the Third World has given him a new E-desire.

There are two objections to (2) that we should consider.

First objection.   It may seem that there is a clear counterexample. Suppose Jones—like St. Paul—has a sudden religious conversion. In the moments after the conversion, he still has conceptions, with respect to each of a variety of expansive self-concepts, about what it would be like to continue to realize the self-concept. This is his attitude toward *being a judge, appreciating good wine, attending the opera, reading contemporary literature,* and so on. These conceptions functioned as motives before his conversion, but they do not do so afterward. The conversion is a clean break with his past; it leaves him totally committed to a new way of life. This is why the conceptions about continuing to realize the self-concepts no longer serve as motives, for they are conceptions about how he could extend his preconversion past into his postconversion future.

Now couldn't this be the case with all of Jones's preconversion self-concepts? More exactly, let c be any expansive self-concept such that, immediately after conversion, Jones has a conception about what it would be like to continue to realize c. Couldn't Jones's break with the past be so complete that, no matter what c is, the conception fails to function as a motive? The idea is that in the moments immediately after his sudden conversion, only his preconversion self-concepts will be such that he has conceptions about what it would be like to continue to realize them. It will be a while before he forms such "could continue" conceptions about his new, postconversion self-concepts. In such a case, (2) entails that Jones is not capable of acting freely; for (2) requires that "could continue" conceptions serve as E-desires.

But is it clear that Jones is unfree in the moments immediately following such a conversion? There are considerations on both sides. On the one hand, there is good reason to regard Jones as incapable of free action. Before conversion, he has a variety of "could continue" conceptions, which serve as unstructured motives. At the moment of conversion, the motivational power of these conceptions is eliminated. The change is immediate and total; he does not reason his way to religious belief; he does not undergo a gradual process of change as his old way of life slowly gives way to a new one. To be held helplessly in the grip of such a change would seem to be the antithesis of being capable of free action.

On the other hand, imagine that in the moments after conversion, Jones has new self-concepts, and he has conceptions of what it would be like to realize—not to continue to realize, but just to realize—these self-concepts. For example, he conceives of himself as realizing the self-concepts: *devoting himself to the imitation of Christ, attending church, studying the Bible*, and so on. Suppose that these conceptions function as E-desires that Jones takes to provide justifications for action, and suppose that he has (and exercises) the ability to act on these E-desires even in the face of opposing desires. Isn't this enough to count Jones as free? Why should it make such a difference whether he conceives of himself as realizing, or as continuing to realize, self-concepts?

Does this show that we were wrong to require, for the ability to act freely, that one should have "could continue" conceptions? The right response here is to retain the requirement and regard the conversion case as a borderline case of being able to act freely (if we regard it as such at all). The reason is that "could continue" conceptions are linked to an essential feature of the ability to act freely: without such conceptions one would not exhibit the independence from the present moment that is an essential feature of freedom. The conversion example actually confirms this point. Suppose that every twenty-four hours Jones undergoes a radical conversion of the sort described in the example. These need not be religious conversions; all that is required is that all preconversion

conceptions about realizing self-conceptions should lose their motivational force and be replaced entirely by conceptions about realizing new self-concepts. Even if we are willing to describe Jones
as able to act freely within each twenty-four-hour period, surely it
is clear that Jones's ability to act freely is seriously impaired. The
shorter the period between conversions, the more serious the im-
pairment to the point whereby, if the periods are sufficiently short—
perhaps five minutes—Jones does not count as capable of free action
at all.

Second objection. The second objection shows that (2) needs
modification. We motivated (2) by pointing out that (1) only partially explicated the sense in which, in free action, the cause of the
action is "in" the agent. However, (2) in turn does not provide a
full explication of "in"-ness. According to (2), the ability to act
freely consists essentially in the ability to exercise a certain control
over one's motives: one can make oneself act on this motive instead
of that one, and one can create and eliminate motives. What (2)
fails to capture is a certain awareness on the part of the agent of
his own motives. In the paradigm case of free action, the agent's
motives are "self-consciously before his mind." This sort of awareness makes one's ability to control his motives effective, for one
has to be aware of what one's motives are to determine whether to
act on this instead of that motive or to determine whether one
should eliminate or create a motive. The claim is that unless one's
control can be effective in this way, one does not have the ability
to act freely.

Before we can argue for this claim, we need to explain it, and
this means answering two questions. What motives are self-
consciously before the mind when one exercises the ability to act
freely? What is meant here by 'self-consciously before the mind'?
To answer the first question, recall that the ability to act freely
consists in a certain ability to act on E-desires. We now need to
explain what it is to act on such a desire; this will reveal just what
motives are involved.

Acting Self-consciously

Suppose that you E-desire to realize the self-concept *playing
chess*. This desire is not a desire to perform any specific action; it

is not, for example, a desire to play this game of chess with Paul. But to act on the desire is to perform some specific action—for example, to play some specific game of chess. So what is the relation between the E-desire and the specific action? There are two cases to distinguish: the case in which the belief is a belief about realization and the case in which the belief is a belief about a means.

Taking the realization case first, suppose that you not only E-desire to realize the self-concept *playing chess*, but you also believe that playing chess with Paul realizes the self-concept. This belief and desire constitute a structured desire you have to play chess with Paul. In playing chess with Paul, you *act on* your E-desire to realize the self-concept *playing chess* if and only if the structured desire is the (or a) cause of your playing. One might think that we should also require that one take the structured desire to be a justification for action. This would yield a narrower notion of acting on a desire, but it turns out that the broader notion that omits any reference to justification is sufficient for our purposes. This definition of acting on a desire is at least in part stipulative, giving a precise sense to 'act on', which we left unexplained initially.

To illustrates the "means" case, suppose that you E-desire to play chess with Paul, and so you plan to spend the weekend with him. You certainly do not believe that spending the weekend realizes the self-concept *playing chess*, but you do believe that spending the weekend is a means to realizing it. This belief and the E-desire form a structured desire to spend the weekend with Paul. In spending the weekend, you are acting on your E-desire to realize the self-concept *playing chess* just in case the structured desire is the (or a) cause of your spending the weekend. This case differs from the realization case in the following way. In the realization case, one acts on a desire to realize a self-concept c, and the action is the action of realizing c; in the means case, the action is not describable as the action of realizing c.

We began this discussion of acting on a desire in order to identify what one has "before one's mind" when one exercises the ability to act freely. We can now say that one is aware of three things: the structured desire and its two components—the desire and the belief of which it consists.[22] The following example illustrates the ways

22. Clearly, one can be aware of the structured desire without being aware of its

in which these items are "before one's mind." Jones is writing a letter to his friend Andreas. When he writes "I hope to see you soon," he is acting on his E-desire to continue to realize the expansive self-concept *expressing friendship*. The structured desire that causes his action consists of this E-desire and the belief that, in writing "I hope to see you soon," he is realizing the self-concept. The structured desire is a desire to realize the self-concept by writing the sentence. In addition, the following three conditions obtain.

(a) The structured desire is a felt desire.

The necessary and sufficient condition of being a felt desire is simply that the desire manifest itself as a feeling of being inclined to act. For example, as the waiter is removing the dishes, you feel yourself inclined to have coffee. This is not to say that there is just one type of felt quality such that every felt desire manifests itself as having that quality; rather, for each felt desire there is some felt quality such that it manifests itself as having that quality.

(b) The E-desire, which is a component of the structured desire, is also a felt desire.

Jones, for example, feels himself inclined to realize the self-concept *expressing friendship*. By 'feel inclined to realize the self-concept *expressing friendship*', I mean what one could also express by 'feel inclined to express friendship'. The reference to the self-concept is not intended to add anything essential. So why make the reference at all? Because in speaking in general about freedom I describe desires as desires to realize this or that self-concept c, and in moving from the general definition of freedom to specific examples, it seems clearest to retain the explicit reference to self-concepts to make it clear just how the example is intended to be a special case of the general definition. Similar remarks apply to my descriptions of beliefs; for example, the belief I describe immediately below as "the belief that writing the sentence realizes the self-

---

components. For example, I can be aware of my structured desire to visit Paul for the weekend without being aware that I desire to play chess with him. I just feel myself inclined to visit. I might even sincerely deny that I want to play chess with Paul.

concept *expressing friendship*" is just the belief that could be described by the sentence "the belief that writing the sentence expresses friendship."

> (c) The third condition concerns the other component of the structured desire—the belief that writing the sentence realizes the self-concept *expressing friendship*. The third condition is that this belief is an occurrent belief.

An occurrent belief is a belief that is before one's mind—in the way that the belief that you are reading this sentence is now before your mind. This is not to say that every occurrent belief is before your mind in *just* the way the belief that you are now reading this sentence is before your mind. An occurrent belief is a belief that manifests itself to consciousness in a way more or less like the way that belief manifests itself. There are distinctions of degree to draw here, for beliefs may linger at the periphery of self-consciousness. For example, early in the day you receive some good news—that you do not need the operation that your doctor first thought you would. For the rest of the day, the belief that the operation is unnecessary lingers on the periphery of self-consciousness. It is not always before your mind in the way that the belief about reading the sentence is, but you have it "in mind" all day. It contrasts in this way with your belief, for example, that Washington, D.C., is the capital of the United States. You are never, during the entire day, aware even in the slightest degree of that belief. Occurrent beliefs form a continuum—from those beliefs that are before one's mind in the way that the belief about reading the sentence is to those beliefs that linger on the periphery of self-consciousness. Similar remarks hold for felt desires, for they, like beliefs, may linger on the periphery of self-consciousness (e.g., on a sunny day, one's desire to sail may, while one is occupied with other activities, linger on the edge of self-consciousness).

Let us express the fact that (a) to (c) are fulfilled by saying that Jones acts *self-consciously* on the E-desire to continue to realize the self-concept *expressing friendship*. What the analysis of freedom given in (2) omits is any reference to acting self-consciously on E-desires. As a first step toward seeing this, consider a continuation of the letter-writing example. When Jones writes "I hope to see you soon," he acts self-consciously on his E-desire to realize the self-concept *expressing friendship*, and with the information in (a) to (c) before his mind, he decides he has already given sufficient expression to his feelings of friendship, so he erases the sentence. It is clear to him that he is beginning to border on the maudlin.

Compare this variant of the example. The overworked Jones is writing the letter to Andreas and listening to a conversation at the same time. In writing the sentence "I hope to see you soon," Jones is acting on his E-desire to continue to realize the self-concept *expressing friendship*, but he does not act self-consciously on the desire. With his mind focused on the conversation, Jones is not even aware of having written the sentence "I hope to see you soon." Indeed, Jones does not notice that he has written the sentence until Smith, reading the letter over Jones's shoulder, asks Jones how he could be so maudlin. Jones explains about the conversation and points out that he was entirely unaware of writing the sentence and that he would not have done it had he been paying attention to what he was doing.

The first point to note here is that, in the second version of the example, Jones could have acted self-consciously, for he has—and had at the time he wrote the sentence—the ability to act self-consciously on his desires. Acting self-consciously is not something that happens to Jones adventitiously. On the contrary, whether he acts self-consciously is under Jones's control: he can make himself so act by exercising his ability to act self-consciously. For example, imagine Jones noticing that he is writing "I hope to see you soon"; he asks himself, "Why am I writing that?" and, prompted to attend to his motives, he has the felt desires and the occurrent belief specified in (a) to (c). In general, Jones—like all of us—is such that attending to his motives typically results in the motives manifesting themselves to consciousness as felt desires and (in the case of structured desires) occurrent beliefs. This does not mean that he can become aware in this way of every motive he has. One's ability to act self-consciously may have a limited scope, extending only to some, not all, of one's motives (as is true if, for example, psychoanalysis is right about the nature of the unconscious; indeed, if psychoanalysis is right the scope may be very limited).

Imagine a creature that satisfies all of the conditions in (2): it has the ability to act on this instead of that E-desire and also has the ability to eliminate and create motives. But suppose that the creature is, so to speak, permanently in the situation that Jones is in the second version of the example; that is, it lacks the ability to act self-consciously on its desires. This is not to say that it never has felt desires or occurrent beliefs, but such awareness is adventitious; it is not something that the creature can make happen.

Does the creature have the ability to act freely? I think not. Effective control of one's motives requires that one be aware of what one's motives are. But as far as such awareness goes, the creature is at the mercy of the adventitious occurrence of its felt desires and occurrent beliefs. The underlying intuition here is again that in free action the source of the action is "in" the agent. Recall the second version of the letter-writing example. Jones treats writing the sentence not so much as something that has its origin "in" him but "outside." He treats it as something that has its origin in the circumstances—in his being overworked, for he contends that had he been acting self-consciously, he would not have written the sentence. To have the ability to act freely is to have the ability to avoid having things forced on one from the "outside" in this way; it is to have to the ability to avoid this by acting self-consciously on one's desires. Free actions have their source "in" one in a way that contrasts with the way in which the source of Jones's writing the sentence is not "in" Jones in the second version of the example.

Further support for this claim comes—again—from the fact that the concept of freedom is part of a network of concepts. The fact that freedom involves the ability to act self-consciously on desires plays an essential role in linking freedom to a special kind of enjoyment and—via the link to enjoyment—to happiness. The fruitfulness of these conceptual connections argues strongly for seeing freedom as involving the ability to act self-consciously on desires.

Having the ability to act freely, then, requires that one have the ability to act self-consciously. There is one further requirement that we should add: the desires on which one has the ability to act self-consciously must be desires to realize self-concepts for their own sake. This may not seem particularly important. After all, we can trace each action undertaken as a means to an end back to some end desired for its own sake. As Aristotle says, "we do not make all our choices for the sake of something else—for in this way the process would go on infinitely so that our desire would be futile and pointless."[23] Having its source in a desire for something for its own sake would not seem to be a distinctive property of a free action. Still, it is worth making it explicit that the desire involved in free action is a desire for something for its own sake, for this allows us to capture another aspect of the sense in which, in the case of free action, the source of the action is 'in oneself'. In addition, the requirement turns out to be essential in connecting freedom to enjoyment.

Consider an example. Jones is visiting friends who, as a special surprise in his honor, take him to their favorite sushi restaurant. Jones, who finds the taste and texture of raw fish just barely tolerable, nonetheless eats the sushi with apparent appreciation and delight. He does so in order not to disappoint his friends, for he E-desires to realize the self-concept *having pleasant times with his friends*. He does not believe that eating raw fish realizes that self-concept, but he does believe that, in the circumstances, it is a means to realizing it. There is a clear sense here in which eating the raw fish is forced on Jones by the circumstances. In this sense, the source of the action does not lie "in" Jones; its source is "foreign"—the working of circumstances that lie beyond Jones's control. But there is another sense in which eating the raw fish does have its source "in" Jones. Jones eats the raw fish as a means to realizing the self-concept *having pleasant times with his friends*, and having a pleasant time with his friends is not something forced on him from the outside by circumstances that dictate the choice of some particular means; he does not want to have a pleasant time with his friends merely as a means to an end. He wants to realize the self-concept for its own sake. So the ultimate source of eating the raw fish does not lie outside Jones in the circumstances but is explained by a desire for something for its own sake.

To state the final analysis, let R be a suitable range of E-desires, where each desire is a desire to continue to realize an expansive self-concept for its own sake and where one takes each desire to provide a justification for action:

> (3) One has the ability to act freely if and only if one has the ability to act self-consciously on each desire in R, even

23. *Nicomachean Ethics*, 1094b20.

when so acting is contrary to one or more of the desires one
does not take to provide justifications.

A final objection.   One may object that (3) leaves out an essential
aspect of freedom. Let R be the suitable range of desires that Smith
takes to provide justifications for action, and suppose that none of
these "takings" is the product of critical reflection and thorough
rational examination. Rather, for each desire in R, Smith's taking
that desire to provide a justification is simply the result of a background of completely unexamined, uncritically accepted beliefs,
attitudes, and prejudices acquired through socialization, upbringing, and the unthinking adoption of the opinions of others. For
short, let us express this by saying that none of Smith's takings are
the product of his own judgement. Surely, the objection goes, Smith
is not free if none of his takings is the product of his own judgment.
How can the source of free action be "in" Smith if his takings are
unthinking adoptions from outside sources?

In answer, we should first note that, even though Smith's takings
are not the product of his own judgment, they could be. This follows
just from the fact that Smith does take desires to be justifications.
To describe Smith as taking a desire to be a justification is to describe him as being in an epistemic state that is responsive to evidence. Smith could consider evidence for and against his takings,
and he could evaluate them in light of this evidence. His takings
would respond to such evaluation; at a minimum, he would abandon those takings that were refuted by the evidence. If he lacks this
ability, he is not properly described as taking a desire to be a justification. So the question before us is not whether we should count
as free a being whose takings could not be the product of his own
judgment but whether we should count as free a being whose takings merely in fact are not the product of his own judgment.

I think we should count such a being as free. The argument that
we should not is that the "in"-ness of the source of action that
typifies freedom requires that one's takings be the product of one's
own judgment. But this ignores that in arguing for (3) we spelled
out a sense in which, if one satisfies (3), the source of free action
is "in" one. The source is "in" one in the sense that one can exercise
a certain kind of rational control over one's motives. Such rational
control does not require that one's takings be the product of one's

own judgment. I contend that this is enough for freedom. This is not to deny that there is an intimate connection between freedom and having one's takings be the product of one's own judgment. One is freer to the extent that one's takings are the product of one's own judgment precisely because one's actions are less dictated by outside sources. But to satisfy (3) is to be—minimally, at least—free.

I have another motive for resisting the suggestion that freedom requires that one's takings be the product of one's own judgment. In the next chapter, I argue that having the ability to act freely is a necessary condition of being a person, and, certainly if sadly, there are many persons whose takings are not the product of their own judgment.

Acting Freely

This completes my discussion of the *ability* to act freely. Now let us turn briefly to the question of what it is to act freely. If one has the ability at a time t to φ, exercising that ability at t is sufficient for φing at t. So a sufficient condition of acting freely is certainly exercising the ability to act freely. Exercising that ability, however, is not a necessary condition of acting freely.

Suppose Jones meets Marilyn and shakes her hand. In shaking her hand, Jones is not—we may suppose—acting on any desire he takes to be a justification for action. He acts without even thinking about it, without even noticing what he is doing. The action is automatic, instilled by years of social interaction. Nonetheless, Jones's shaking hands with Marilyn is not done unfreely; on the contrary, it is under his control, for he could have exercised his ability to act freely at the time of the action. He could have asked himself whether shaking Marilyn's hand conflicted with any of the desires he takes to be justifications for action. Had he decided it did, he could have exercised his ability to act freely so as to make himself do something other than shake Marilyn's hand. Shaking her hand is an action that it is within Jones's power to perform or not, accordingly as it is or is not compatible with acting on those desires that he takes to provide justifications. One more example: Smith insults Jones. Jones, angered, strikes him. His anger makes him S-desire to hit Smith, and he acts on that desire. If this desire overpowers him and deprives him of his ability to act on his E-desires, Jones does not act freely. If, however, he retains the ability, he does act freely. In such a case, he could determine whether striking Smith was contrary to some E-desire he took to justification for action; if he determined that it was, he could act on that E-desire instead of his S-desire.

It makes good sense to count such actions as free, for the underlying idea behind the account of the ability to act freely is that to have that ability is to have the ability to control one's actions in a certain way. Jones's shaking Marilyn's hand is not controlled by Jones in the sense of being a product of Jones's exercising his ability to act freely, but it does not lie entirely outside the reach of such control since Jones could have exercised his ability with respect to that action. In general, we can distinguish two classes of actions. The first consists of actions performed when the agent lacks the ability to act freely. Such actions are not under the agent's control in the way that Jones's shaking Marilyn's hand is under Jones's control. The second class consists of actions performed when the agent has the ability to act freely. These actions are under the agent's control in the relevant way and count as free.

Let us turn to the question of what it is to be a person.

3 Personhood

What is it to be a person? An Aristotelian assumption underlies my answer: each kind of living being—persons included—is associated with an ordered pattern of change and behavior. A being counts as one and the same kind of thing over time by virtue of exhibiting the pattern associated with that kind.[1] Furthermore, an informative account of what it is to be a thing of a certain kind K can be given by specifying the ordered pattern associated with K. These assumptions are widely (although not universally) shared, and I will not argue for them. They are, however, worth illustrating.

Consider a tiger. It exhibits a spatiotemporally continuous pattern of change and behavior from birth into adulthood and finally se-

---

1. This conception has recently been extensively articulated by David Wiggins, *Sameness and Substance* (Cambridge: Harvard University Press, 1980). This conception of objects plays a central role in contemporary biology. See, for example, C. H. Waddington, "The Human Animal," in *The Evolution of an Evolutionist* (Ithaca, N.Y.: Cornell University Press, 1975), p. 268: "The most important point is an extremely general one, namely that all biological organization, whether of cells, individual organisms or populations, is involved in temporal change. Life is through and through a dynamic process." (In assuming that persons are no exception to this general fact, I am dismissing "pure ego" theories of personal identity and more generally what C. D. Broad calls "Centre Theories" in *The Mind and Its Place in Nature* [London: Routledge and Kegan Paul, 1925], p. 558f. See Colin McGinn, *The Character of Mind* [Oxford: Oxford University Press, 1982], p. 111f., for a position more akin than mine to a "pure ego" view.)

nescence. All normal tigers go through the same changes in (approximately) the same order and behave in approximately the same ways; the developmental pattern ceases with adulthood, but a characteristic behavioral pattern persists. We count the adult tiger and the cub from which it developed as one and the same tiger, and we do so at least in part because the change from cub to adult exemplifies the pattern of change and behavior characteristic of tigers: the order establishes a unity.[2] Moreover, the order would seem to be not just sufficient but also necessary to unity over time; if a tiger deviates—significantly—from this order (e.g., it explodes), the tiger ceases to exist. As to what counts as a significant deviation, there is no need to give a precise answer—if indeed such an answer is possible. It is enough to note that as deviations from the normal order become more pronounced, we are more and more inclined to think that the tiger ceases to exist.

The same pattern of change and behavior that establishes unity over time serves as a standard that defines (at least in part) our concept of a normal tiger: to be a tiger is to be the kind of thing that—normally—exhibits a certain pattern of change and behavior. This connection between pattern and concept is the reason an informative account of what it is to be a thing of a certain kind K can be given by specifying the ordered pattern associated with K. To illustrate the connection, suppose that, through special techniques, we accelerate the development of a tiger embryo so that it develops into an adult tiger in a week; imagine that the order as well as the speed of development is altered (the accelerated development is not simply like a film of regular development run at very high speed). If what we produce is really a tiger, it must be true that it (or something qualitatively identical with it in all important respects[3]) could have developed in the normal way. Otherwise, how could the thing we produce be a tiger?

2. One might think that the pattern of change and behavior should be specified at a more "basic level"—for example, in terms of DNA—but the level does not matter; the point is that for each kind of object, there is a pattern of change and behavior, where things of that kind count as the same thing over time by virtue of exemplifying that pattern. This claim is independent of any decision about the appropriate level at which to describe such patterns.

3. I said "in all important respects" because the artificially developed tiger would still be a real tiger even if, for example, the particular shade of its coat was

But what is the characteristic pattern of change and behavior associated with persons? Answers typically begin with one of two intuitions: that personal identity over time is essentially a matter of a pattern in one's mental life or that the relevant pattern is a pattern of change and behavior exhibited by the body. Theories that begin with the first intuition ultimately have to concede that the body plays an important role in personal identity; theories that begin with the second one have to concede that the mental matters a great deal. It suits my purposes best to begin with the first intuition; later, I point out where the body becomes essential.

The Typical Pattern

The relevant unity-establishing order in one's mental life is the result of exercising one's ability to act freely. This is the distinctive feature of the theory I offer. The theory contrasts with more "passive" mental-continuity theories of personal identity—in particular with memory theories like Locke's.[4] In memory theories, the order over time that makes one a person is not actively imposed by the person himself; it is just a question of whether there is a memory-connection of the right sort. I will argue for my "active" account of personal identity by first describing a way in which persons typically use their ability to act freely—a way that establishes a certain order in their mental life. Then I will argue that this is not only typically but also necessarily the case.

As an example of the typical use, suppose that Edwards E-desires to continue to realize each self-concept in the collection of expansive self-concepts C; C includes *being a doctor, sailing frequently, vacationing in interesting places, enjoying good wine,* and *educating her children.* Note that the concepts are expansive self-concepts—concepts that require (or permit) realization over time. This is why Edwards, in trying to realize these self-concepts, sched-

---

a result of its artificial development and never occurred in the normal process of development.

4. John Locke, *An Essay Concerning Human Understanding,* 2d ed. (1694), chap. 27. The most plausible such theory is Paul Grice's; see H. P. Grice, "Personal Identity," *Mind,* 50 (October 1941). Grice's theory is carefully discussed and partially defended by John Perry, "Personal Identity, Memory, and the Problem of Circularity," in John Perry, ed., *Personal Identity* (Berkeley: University of California Press, 1975).

ules their realization in a particular order over time, devoting some time to this self-concept, some time to that one, some time to another one, and so on: for example, she takes a vacation to sail for two weeks and to visit her daughter at her college; then she returns to her medical practice; later she visits her son over a long weekend.

Let us focus on Edwards's visiting her son. She is, in making the visit, acting on her E-desire to continue to realize the self-concept *educating her children*. To act on an E-desire is to be caused to act by a structured desire consisting of the E-desire and a belief. The relevant belief in this case is Edwards's belief that the visit realizes the self-concept; this belief and the E-desire form the structured desire to visit her son. Note that the E-desire is a relatively permanent feature of Edwards's motivational structure; it persists in her over a relatively long period. The belief, on the other hand, is a transient feature of her motivational makeup. It is formed in response to the arrival of the long weekend and figures as a motivational factor only for the duration of her visit to her son.

In general, Edwards has an array of standing E-desires to realize self-concepts. These E-desires are motivating conceptions—collections of thoughts about what it would be like to realize the self-concept. More exactly, they are collections of thoughts about what it would be like *to continue* to realize the self-concept, for the conceptions that motivate Edwards represent her as having in the past realized this or that expansive self-concept and as continuing to do so in the future. Beliefs arise about which experiences and activities might realize these self-concepts, and some of these beliefs combine with her E-desires to form structured desires. This is not to say that she automatically acts on these desires. On the contrary, when she visits her son over the long weekend, she also believes that flying to Hawaii would realize the self-concept *vacationing in interesting places*, and this belief and her E-desire to continue to realize that self-concept combine to form a structured desire to fly to Hawaii. But she does not act on this desire. Nor does she act on the very strong S-desire to spend the weekend lying on the beach.

The explanation of Edwards's behavior has two parts. (1) Edwards is in general such that she will exercise her ability to act freely to ensure that she acts—sufficiently often—on E-desires to continue to realize the expansive self-concepts in the collection *C*. Put aside for the moment the obscurity of the phrase 'sufficiently often'. (2) Edwards E-desires to realize the self-concept *educating her children*, and she exercises her ability to act freely to (try to) ensure that she acts on the desire to educate her children instead of the desire to fly to Hawaii or the desire to lie on the beach.

Let us express (1) by saying that Edwards is *committed* to realizing the self-concepts in C sufficiently often. The notion of commitment plays a central role both in the analysis of personhood and in the analysis of leading a happy life, and for this reason, we need a fuller explanation of what commitment is. To this end, recall that among the self-concepts to which Edwards is committed are *being a doctor, sailing frequently, vacationing in interesting places, enjoying good wine*, and *educating her children*. But Edwards cannot simply go sailing, vacation, or drink wine as the opportunity arises, not if she is also to maintain a medical practice and use the income therefrom to educate her children. To have reasonable prospects of realizing all the self-concepts in C sufficiently often, she must schedule the realization of those self-concepts over time. She does this by forming, and acting in accord with, certain beliefs. For example, she believes that it will be conducive to realizing her self-concepts sufficiently often if she vacations for two weeks, visits her daughter at her college at the end of that vacation, and then returns to her medical practice.[5] Edwards exercises her ability to act freely as necessary to ensure that she acts on her E-desires in the order specified in such beliefs. This does not mean that Edwards will always exercise her ability to act in accord with such an order; sudden unexpected opportunities may arise that lead her to abandon the envisioned order. Or there may be no need to exercise her ability to act freely, for she may find herself acting in accord with the order specified in her beliefs, with no opposing desires to overcome. On the other hand, if there is an opposing desire, she may be overpowered by it and so be deprived of the ability to act freely. Or she may simply fail to exercise the ability through inattention, laziness, carelessness, distraction, hypnotic trance, drugged states, disease, and so on.

To give a general definition of commitment, let C* be a collection

5. Of course, I am not saying that Edwards would express this belief using the words 'realizing self-concepts sufficiently often'; my point is that she has a belief that we can describe in this way.

of expansive self-concepts where one E-desires to realize each self-concept in C^*. Then, during a certain period of time

> one is committed to realizing the self-concepts in C^* sufficiently often if and only if, during that period
>
> (1) one regularly forms beliefs as to how to realize those self-concepts sufficiently often; and
> (2) during that period—barring eventualities such as lack of need, unexpected opportunity, inattention, carelessness, being overpowered by a desire, and so on—one exercises one's ability to act freely to (try to) ensure that one acts on one's E-desires in the order specified in such beliefs.

Two points are in order. First, (2) entails that the E-desires to realize the self-concepts in C^* are desires that one takes to be justifications for realizing those self-concepts; otherwise, one could not exercise one's ability to act freely to ensure that one acts on those desires since the ability to act freely is the ability to act on desires that one takes to provide justifications for action. (This will be important in Chapter 5 when we discuss happiness.) The second point concerns the meaning of 'regularly' in "regularly forms beliefs"; the meaning is that such belief formation is a frequent, nonsporadic feature of one's life—how frequent is a question I will take up later.

A question I will not postpone is the question of what 'sufficiently often' means. The idea is that, in the case of Edwards, for example, there is a certain frequency of realization such that Edwards will exercise her ability to act freely as she takes it to be necessary to do so in order to realize her self-concepts *that* frequently. The frequency may vary from person to person, but given that a person is committed to realizing self-concepts, there is some frequency of realization such that the person will exercise his ability to act freely as he takes it to be necessary to do so to realize his self-concepts *that* frequently. The frequency of realization involved here may not be specifiable in any precise way, but this is no objection to thinking that there is a certain roughly and approximately specifiable frequency involved. Think of the frequency as an approximately specifiable range of (precisely specifiable) frequencies, a range with an upper and lower bounds that themselves may be vague and only approximately specifiable. In addition, this frequency may be a "weighted" frequency in the sense that realizing some self-concepts may take precedence over realizing others; for example, for Edwards *educating her children* might take precedence over *enjoying good wine.* Thus suppose that Edwards has been so busy during a certain period that although she has seen to the education of her children, she has had no time for wine drinking; nonetheless, she regards herself as having realized the self-concept in C sufficiently often. She would not have this attitude—let us suppose—if there had been no time to devote to the education of her children but there had been opportunities to drink good wine. Whether she counts as realizing his self-concepts sufficiently often is in part a function of which concepts take precedence over others.[6]

These remarks should suffice for an explanation of the idea of commitment—or almost. It is also worth remarking on a connection with the notion, discussed in Chapter 1, of a susceptibility to motivation. This connection is simply that to be committed to realizing self-concepts *is* to have a certain susceptibility to motivation by conceptions; one is susceptible to motivation by conceptions that articulate ways to realize one's self-conceptions sufficiently often. This is not to say that commitment is the only source of susceptibility to motivation; it is, however, one important source.

More important, *it is by virtue of being committed to realizing a collection of self-concepts sufficiently often that one imposes a certain order over time on one's mental life.* Consider Edwards again. Because she is committed to realizing the expansive self-concepts in C, her thoughts and actions combine to yield a temporally extended series of experiences and activities that realize expansive self-concepts, for she regularly forms beliefs as to how to realize these self-concepts sufficiently often, and she exercises her ability to act freely to ensure that she realizes her self-concepts in accord with the order specified in those beliefs. This claim requires some qualification. Edwards may be committed to the self-concepts in C; yet her thoughts and actions may nonetheless fail to combine in the described way. There are two possibilities.

6. I do not mean to imply that a collection C of self-concepts is, or must be, ordered in any particular way; such a collection may exemplify a variety of different order relations, and the relations it exemplifies need not order the whole set or the same parts of the set. Moreover, the collection may not be ordered at all. My explication of "sufficiently often" as possibly involving a "weighted frequency" is intended to be abstract enough to encompass all possibilities.

First possibility.   Edwards may not have the opportunity to act in accord with these beliefs. Suppose that, just as she is planning her vacation, she is drafted into the army and sent to El Salvador where she is taken prisoner and held captive for twenty years. Still, within the constraints imposed by others, her life will exhibit a certain order by virtue of her commitment to realizing self-concepts. As a prisoner, she will conduct herself in this way or that—cooperative or defiant, say—according to her commitment to self-concepts. In general, she will form beliefs about how to realize her self-concepts sufficiently often. In the circumstances, she may not believe that she will succeed in realizing those self-concepts sufficiently often, but she will form beliefs about how to approximate to that goal. To describe these two possibilities, it is convenient to introduce some special terminology. Thus, in what follows, I will use 'beliefs as to how to realize one's self-concepts sufficiently often' to cover both the case in which one believes that one will (or is likely to) realize one's self-concepts sufficiently often and the case in which one thinks that the best one can do is some (possibly very remote) approximation. This is not to say that the difference is unimportant. On the contrary, I will argue later that one is leading a happy life only if one expects to continue to realize one's self-concepts sufficiently often.

Second possibility.   Certain of Edwards's beliefs may be false. There are two cases to consider here. In the first, Edwards believes, and acts in accord with the belief, that it will be conducive to realizing her self-concepts sufficiently often if she vacations for two weeks, visits her daughter at her college at the end of that vacation, and then returns to her medical practice. This belief could be false. It could turn out that she spent too much time vacationing with the result that she has to work especially hard at her medical practice to make up the lost time; this could mean that she has to forgo realizing other concepts to such an extent that, for a certain period, she is not realizing her self-concepts sufficiently often. But even in such a case, Edwards's life exhibits a certain order. When she acts on the false belief, her thoughts and actions still combine in a certain way—in a way that she *believes* will realize her self-concepts sufficiently often; when she works especially hard at her medical practice to make up for lost time, her thoughts and actions combine in a way that she thinks will—in the long run—be conducive to realizing her self-concepts sufficiently often.

The second case is concerned not with beliefs as to how to realize self-concepts sufficiently often but with another kind of belief: E-desires, they being, after all, motivating conceptions. We explained a conception as a complex of thoughts, and we used 'thought' to cover both the mere entertaining of an idea as well as a belief. It is the belief case that concerns us here. The E-desires/conceptions that we are concerned with are beliefs about what it would be like to continue to realize expansive self-concepts. To have such a "could continue" belief is, in part, to believe that one has in the past realized the self-concept in question. But what if the "could continue" beliefs involved in Edwards's E-desires are all, or almost all, false? For example, Edwards believes that she could continue to realize the self-concept *enjoying good wine*, but contrary to what she believes, it is false that she has ever realized that concept in the past. Edwards has been brainwashed, and the past she thinks she had is not the past she really had. In such a case, Edwards will not really be continuing a series begun in the past when she acts on her E-desires, and her life will fail to exhibit the self-concept-realizing order over time.

In response, let me first make a certain assumption explicit: the conditions under which Edwards lives her life do not depart too far from *ideal conditions of freedom*. Ideal conditions of freedom obtain for one during a given period of time just in case (1) one can, during that time, remember all the experiences and activities that realized (or that one believed realized) one's self-concepts; and (2) one has the ability to act on any E-desire that one has. Ideal conditions of freedom rarely, if ever, obtain. Ordinarily at least, one cannot remember every self-concept-realizing experience or activity, and one does not have the ability to act on every E-desire one has. However, all (or most) of us live our lives under conditions that approximate to ideal conditions of freedom. For example, Edwards will be able to remember—that is, have memory-knowledge of—a number of her self-concept-realizing experiences and activities, so the beliefs that constitute her E-desires will on the whole be true. Moreover, although Edwards may not have the ability to act on each E-desire that she has, she will—by virtue of having the ability to act freely—have the ability to act on a suitable range of such desires, and as a result, she will, through exercising her ability to act freely, be able to generate a series of experiences and activities that realizes expansive self-concepts.

These are the points I will express by saying that Edwards lives under conditions that do not depart *too far* from ideal conditions of freedom. I will take up the question of how far is too far later. The point I want to emphasize now is that if one lives one's life under conditions that do not depart too far from ideal conditions of freedom, then, given that one is committed to realizing a collection of expansive self-concepts sufficiently often, one's thoughts and actions will combine over time to produce a self-concept-realizing series of experiences and activities. Typically, a person's life exhibits this self-imposed, self-concept-realizing order since—typically—persons are committed to realizing a collection of expansive self-concepts sufficiently often and live under conditions that do not depart too far from ideal conditions of freedom.

What is typically true is in fact necessarily true. It may seem that there is an obvious counterexample to this claim, and we can see why the claim is true by seeing why the apparent counterexample is merely apparent.[7]

The Necessary Pattern

The apparent counterexample: Jones wearies of the constant making of decisions that daily life entails, so he hires a group of people—The Deciders—to make all his decisions for him.[8] He does anything and everything they tell him to do. Isn't this a case in which Jones is a person but not committed to realizing any particular collection of self-concepts sufficiently often? The answer depends on how the example is filled out. To begin with, what is Jones's attitude toward The Deciders? One possibility is that he is committed to realizing the self-concept *doing what The Deciders say*; this would explain why he does everything they tell him to do. This is a natural way to think of the example, for Jones makes one last decision: to submit himself to The Deciders; it is natural to think of him as abiding by

7. The discussion that follows owes a great deal to a conversation with Paul Grice; I am also indebted here to Andreas Esheté, with whom I have extensively discussed examples such as those that follow.

8. The phrase 'The Deciders' is Paul Grice's invention.

this decision because he is committed to the self-concept, *doing what The Deciders say*. But, of course, this would not be a case in which Jones is entirely uncommitted to realizing self-concepts.

To avoid this difficulty, let us suppose that Jones never decides to submit himself to The Deciders. They have overseen him from birth, and Jones has from his earliest moments gone along with what they want. Think of Jones as a child-king and of The Deciders as his regents. Miniature transmitters have been implanted in Jones's nervous system so that all of his sensory input is relayed to The Deciders' computer (programmed by The Deciders to control Jones just in the way they desire). The Deciders leave minor decisions—where to eat lunch, when to go to bed, and so on—entirely to the computer, but there is always at least one Decider on duty to handle major decisions. Jones never challenges the decisions of The Deciders; it never occurs to him to raise the question of whether he should go along with what they say; he just does. Here we do not have to think of Jones as committed to realizing the self-concept *doing what The Deciders say*. Instead, we may suppose that The Deciders control Jones by implanting desires in him (through miniature receivers implanted in Jones's nervous system). The implanted desires are so strong that they are always the ones that cause Jones to act. Isn't this a case in which Jones is a person but in which he has no commitment to realizing self-concepts sufficiently often? Yes, but the reason for the yes means that the "counterexample" does not constitute an objection to the proposed condition.

The first point is that persons—like all living beings—are associated with a pattern of change and behavior over time; so, if, in the purported counterexample, it is to be plausible that Jones is a person, it must be plausible that he exhibits the relevant order. One way to make this plausible is to think of The Deciders as ensuring that Jones's life exhibits (or could exhibit) the sort of ordered pattern of change and behavior that is *typical* of persons—the *self-imposed*, self-concept-realizing order illustrated by the Edwards example. Unlike Edwards, Jones does not impose this order on his life himself by exercising the ability to act freely; rather, The Deciders are the source of the order. Nonetheless, by virtue of the surrogate order provided by The Deciders, Jones's thoughts and actions approximate very closely to what is typical.

If the provision by The Deciders of this surrogate order is essential to its being plausible that Jones is a person, the example is not an objection to the proposed necessary condition. In such a case, Jones counts as person only because he approximates to what the condition requires—a condition that is typically fulfilled. Against such a background of typical cases, we should recognize Jones as a borderline case because he is otherwise like a normal person, even to the point where his life exhibits a surrogate of the self-imposed, self-concept-realizing order; and because had things been a little different—that is, no Deciders—he would have fulfilled the necessary condition. But all of this is predicated on the assumption that the provision, by The Deciders, of this surrogate order is essential to its being plausible that Jones is a person. What if Jones's life does not exhibit the surrogate order? Suppose The Deciders amuse themselves by seeing how disordered a life they can impose on Jones so that the unfortunate Jones never sticks to any one activity for long; he jumps from one activity to another in an apparently senseless and aimless way. Is this Jones a person? A question in reply: Does Jones have the ability to act freely? He never exercises the ability since he is completely controlled by The Deciders. But does he possess the ability? The answer to this question will reveal whether Jones counts as a person. There are three cases to distinguish.

1. Jones does possess the ability, and he could, by exercising the ability, resist the dictates of The Deciders and make himself act on desires other than those that they implant. But Jones never tries to resist; the thought never even occurs to him. In this case, Jones is a person—albeit an unfortunate one. He is like a person who has been given a drug that powerfully inclines him to engage in a series of disconnected, random activities. He could resist the effects of the drug, but he does not. The drug sufferer is still a person; after all, before taking the drug, his life exhibited the self-concept-realizing order typical of persons; it will do so again when the drug wears off, and it could do so even while he is under the influence of the drug. Jones differs from the drug sufferer in that Jones's life (we are now supposing) never has, and never will, exhibit the self-concept-realizing order typical of persons; however, he is like the drug sufferer in that his life could exhibit this order if he would just resist The Deciders. This would seem to be enough to secure that Jones is a person.

2. Jones lacks the ability to act freely but would have it if it were

not for the intervention of The Deciders. They have deprived him of it by implanting electrodes in his brain and can restore the ability by removing the electrodes. This case is very much like the first one except that Jones is not like the drug sufferer who could resist the drug but is like a person who, because of reversible brain damage, has temporarily lost the ability to act freely. Before the brain damage, the person's life exhibited the self-concept-realizing order typical of persons, and it will again exhibit this order upon recovery. This is sufficient to secure that the sufferer of the brain damage is a person. Jones differs from this person in that Jones's life has not exhibited, and never will exhibit, a self-concept-realizing order. Still, it would exhibit this order if The Deciders would release their hold, and—perhaps—this would seem enough to count Jones as a person. At least let us grant, for the sake of argument, that it is.

3. The Deciders permanently and irreversibly deprive Jones of the ability to act freely. In this case, I take it to be clear that Jones is not a person, for I take it to be clear that having the ability to act freely—or, at least, being such that one normally has that ability—is a necessary condition of being a person. Without this ability, Jones is just some strange creature The Deciders have wired up for their amusement—a sort of biological robot. The reason for this lies in this observation of Frankfurt:

> ... the criteria for being a person do not serve primarily to distinguish the members of our own species from the members of other species. Rather, they are designed to capture those attributes which are the subject of our most humane concern with ourselves and the source of what we regard as most important and problematical in our lives. Now these attributes would be of equal significance to us even if they were not in fact peculiar and common to the members of our own species. What interests us most in the human condition would not interest us less if it were also a feature of the condition of other creatures as well.... Our concept of ourselves as a person is not to be understood, therefore, as a concept of attributes that are necessarily species specific.[9]

The ability to act freely is an attribute that could be possessed by members of other species and is certainly "the subject of our most humane concern with ourselves and the—or, at least, a major—

9. Harry G. Frankfurt, "Freedom of the Will," in Gary Watson, ed., *Free Will* (Oxford: Oxford University Press, 1982), p. 82.

source of "what we regard as most important and problematical in our lives." This is good reason to think it is criterial of personhood. What other nonspecies specific attribute could fill the bill?

So: whether Jones has the ability to act freely makes all the difference as to whether he counts as a person. But if possession of the ability makes all the difference, possession of that ability must be related in some way to exemplifying the ordered pattern of change and behavior associated with persons. Mere possession of the ability will not secure that one's life exhibits any particular order; one must exercise the ability. But merely exercising the ability is not enough to ensure that one's life exhibits a certain order; the exercise must be directed toward some end. I submit that the end is realizing self-concepts sufficiently often, or more exactly: realizing the expansive self-concepts in a collection C sufficiently often, C being the collection to which one is committed. Part of being so committed is regularly forming beliefs as to how to realize the self-concepts in C sufficiently often. These beliefs serve to guide the exercise of the ability to act freely so that over time one imposes the self-concept-realizing order on one's thought and action. This order appears in all the typical cases, and there is certainly a presumption that the order that appears in the typical cases is the ordered pattern of change and behavior by virtue of which one counts as one and the same person over time.

So we again have the result that the example of The Deciders is not an objection to the proposed necessary condition. In case 3 Jones is not a person, and it turns out that, in cases 1 and 2, in which Jones (perhaps) does count as person, he does so only because he would meet the condition if circumstances were different. In those cases, we may legitimately recognize Jones as a (borderline) case of being a person while still holding the suggested condition to be necessary.

Why not take the suggested condition to be sufficient as well as necessary? Why not simply say that one is a person *if* and only if there is a collection C of expansive self-concepts that one is committed to realizing sufficiently often? The answer is that this may well be a necessary and sufficient condition of being a person; it is indeed difficult to think of any convincing counterexamples. But the account should be necessary, sufficient, *and* informative, and the current suggested condition is not informative enough about what it is to be a person.

To see why, consider that a commitment to realizing self-concepts is generally only a commitment for a period of time. Commitments change with time; for example, when Edwards's son and daughter both graduate from college, the self-concept *educating her children* may well cease to be among the self-concepts to which Edwards is committed. What this means is that we have not fully specified the ordered pattern over time that is associated with persons. The self-concept-realizing order generated by commitment to self-concepts is only one component of this order.

This is illustrated well by the case of M. Alphonse Ratisbonne, a Jew and a free thinker, who had a vision of the Virgin Mary that converted him to Catholicism. He describes his state of mind just after the vision as follows:

> I did not know where I was: I did not know whether I was Alphonse or another. I only felt myself changed and believed myself another me; I looked for myself in myself and did not find myself. In the bottom of my soul I felt an explosion of the most ardent joy; I could not speak; I had no wish to reveal what had happened.... I came out as from a living sepulchre, from an abyss of darkness; and I was living, perfectly living. But I wept, for at the bottom of that gulf I saw the extreme misery from which I had been saved by an infinite mercy.[10]

Before conversion, Alphonse was committed to realizing one collection of self-concepts; after conversion, to another, different collection. Because of these commitments, Alphonse's thought and action exemplify the self-imposed, self-concept-realizing order both before and after conversion, and (borderline cases aside) he would not count as a person if he did not exhibit this order. But the moment of conversion marks a sharp discontinuity in this order, for at that point the self-concepts involved alter dramatically. Nonetheless, the postconversion Alphonse is still the same person as the preconversion Alphonse. But the "two" Alphonses count as the same person only if they are connected by the right sort of ordered pattern of change and behavior over time. What ordered pattern is this? It cannot be the ordered pattern that is the result of commitment to this or that specific set of self-concepts because no one pattern of this sort links the preconversion and postconversion Alphonses; the

10. The case is reported by William James, *The Varieties of Religious Experience* (New York: The Modern Library, 1946), p. 221.

preconversion pattern ceases at the moment of conversion, and the new pattern begins only after conversion. Yet these patterns are components of the pattern of change and behavior associated with persons, so there must be some broader, overall pattern in which the preconversion and postconversion self-concept-realizing orders are embedded.

The Necessary and Sufficient Pattern

To describe this overall pattern, let us return to the case of Edwards and describe what is typically true—again with the intention of arguing that what is typically true is also necessarily true. Consider the total span of time during which the person Edwards exists. Let the following line represent this span of time:

$$T$$

This totality can be divided into parts:

$$T_1 \quad T_2 \quad T_3 \qquad \ldots \qquad T_n$$

For each T_i there is a collection of expansive self-concepts C such that, throughout T_i, Edwards is committed to using her ability to act freely to realize the expansive self-concepts in C sufficiently often. Moreover, each T_i is a maximal period of time during which Edwards is committed to the expansive self-concepts in C. To define 'maximal', suppose that the moment of time t is in the period of time T_i, and let t^* be a moment of time that immediately precedes or immediately follows t, where Edwards is committed to realizing the concepts in C at t^*. T_i is a maximal period of commitment if and only if each such t^* is in T_i.

Typically, there will be some vagueness about where one T_i ends and another begins. But there need not be. Suppose Edwards's daughter and then her son graduate from college. It is certainly possible that Edwards should cease to be committed to the self-concept *educating her children* at the precise moment she sees her son handed his diploma. Typically, however, commitments change slowly: for example, as Edwards grows older, she spends more and more time on her medical practice, and her commitment to vacationing slowly fades until it is entirely gone; a commitment to reading the medical journals grows slowly as the other commitment fades. The causes of change from one period of commitment to another are heterogeneous. There are the various forms of social conditioning and pressure—from one's upbringing and education to television commercials; there are the psychological dynamics of one's own character as it develops and matures; there are the demands of one's job, the books one reads, one's friends, one's spouse, one's children, and so on.

Such changes typically occur under conditions that do not depart too far from ideal conditions of freedom. That is, changes occur when one can remember, to a considerable extent, those past experiences and activities that realized (or that one believed realized) self-concepts and when one has the ability to act on a considerable range of one's E-desires. This means that a person has a certain degree of control over changes in his commitment to realizing self-concepts, for he can resist changes in his commitment to realizing self-concepts.

Consider an example. You are comtemplating becoming a bon-vivant. The idea seems preposterous at first, but your imagination keeps returning to and playing with the idea until a detailed conception—an elaborate complex of thoughts about what it would be like to realize the self-concept—slowly grows around the idea. You are particularly susceptible to motivation by conceptions that represent you as devil-may-care, and for this reason, this particular conception is not motivationally inert but serves as an E-desire to realize the self-concept *being a bon-vivant*. Indeed, you are on the verge of having the concept *being a bon-vivant* included in the collection of expansive self-concepts that you are committed to realizing. But you decide to avoid commitment to that self-concept since you think such a commitment would diminish the time you have to spend on realizing another concept to which you are already committed—*training for the Olympics*. Commitment to *being a bon-vivant* would, you decide, make your training much less effective. Given that conditions do not depart too far from ideal conditions of freedom, there are two ways in which you can resist such a commitment. (1) Whenever you are tempted to act on your E-desire to realize the self-concept *being a bon-vivant*, you exercise your ability to act freely so as to act on another E-desire instead, for example, the E-desire to realize the self-concept *training for the Olympics*. (2) You make yourself think carefully and honestly about what it would really be like to be a bon-vivant. This leads you to question and then finally abandon your initial conception of what it would be like to realize that self-concept. Since the motivation to realize that self-concept was supplied by that conception, you cease to be motivated.[11]

In general, under conditions that do not depart too far from ideal conditions of freedom, commitments to realizing self-concepts are relatively self-preserving. One can resist changes in one's commitment to certain self-concepts, and—precisely because one is committed to realizing just those self-concepts and not others—one will tend to resist such changes. This does not mean that change will not occur. For example, when *educating her children* ceases to be among the concepts to which Edwards is committed, it need not be the case that she has the ability to resist that particular change. Edwards's particular attitudes toward educating her children could be so deeply ingrained in her character that she could not, upon seeing her son handed his diploma, have resisted ceasing to be committed to that self-concept. In general, the ability to resist changes in one's commitment to self-concepts is a matter of degree. A child is able to do this to a lesser degree than an adult; adults vary in the degree to which they are able to do so, and the same adult may at different times vary in the degree to which he is able to do so. Still, given conditions that do not depart too far from ideal conditions of freedom, commitments will be *relatively* self-preserving, and this means that change will, as a rule, be gradual and continuous—as illustrated by Edwards's gradually acquiring a commitment to reading the medical journals while slowly losing her commitment to vacationing.

To get an overall picture of such change, consider the total span of time T during which Edwards exists:

11. Compare the avoiding-the-illusion-of-youthfulness example from Chapter 2, in which Smith decides that it is false that he could realize the self-concept *having a young lover*.

During any particular T_i, Edwards's thoughts and actions will exhibit the self-imposed, self-concept realizing order. Since this is true for each T_i, Edwards's life *as a whole* will exhibit a certain order. Consider any two adjacent periods T_i and T_{i+1}. During T_i Edwards's mental life will exhibit the self-imposed, self-concept-realizing order, and this will be true of T_{i+1} as well. The self-concepts involved will be different, but since the change from T_i to T_{i+1} occurs under conditions that do not depart too far from ideal conditions of freedom, the T_i-order and the T_{i+1}-order will—typically—merge gradually into one another. My claim is that

> one is a person if and only if the total period of time T during which one exists divides into periods $T_1, \ldots, T_n$ such that each T_i is a maximal period of commitment, and throughout T conditions never depart too far from ideal conditions of freedom.

Why accept this account? The main reason is that cases of extreme departure from ideal conditions of freedom turn out to be clear cases in which personal identity over time is not preserved.

For example, Smith, who is working as a spy, is committed to realizing a collection C of self-concepts, where C includes *being a spy for the United States, being loyal to the United States, never cooperating with the Soviets*, and the like. Smith is captured and subjected to brainwashing. The goal is to eliminate his commitment to the self-concepts in C and replace it with a commitment to the self-concepts in C^*, where C^* includes concepts such as *being a spy for the USSR* and *being loyal to the USSR*. Smith proves extremely resistant to this replacement, for he retains his memories, character traits, patterns of emotional response, personal loyalties, and various beliefs, hopes, fears, desires, and so on; these psychological features support him in his commitment to C and make him resist any commitment to C^*. To overcome this barrier, Smith's captors wipe Smith's mind clean, as it were; they implant entirely new and different "memories," character traits, patterns of emotional response, personal loyalties, beliefs, hopes, fears, desires, and so on. The final result is a person—call him the 'after-person'—who is committed to realizing the self-concepts in C^*. Smith is not the same person as the after-person, for—and I take this to be clear—the person Smith no longer exists. Permanent elimination of all memories and permanent alteration of all character traits, patterns of emotional response, personal loyalties, beliefs, hopes, fears, desires, and so on is sufficient to eliminate the person Smith from existence.

The essential point is that this example is a case of a radical departure from ideal conditions of freedom: Smith loses his memory, and he is deprived of his ability to act freely when he is in the hands of his captors. What the example illustrates is that cases involving this radical a departure from ideal conditions of freedom are cases in which personal identity is not preserved. But how radical a departure is required before personal identity is not preserved? Suppose, for example, that the police bring Smith into the hospital emergency room; they found him running naked down one of the city's main streets. Smith insists that his thoughts, impulses, and actions are controlled by beings from outer space, the Zircons. The Zircons communicate with him by mental telepathy, and he submits passively to their commands. The Zircons commanded him to run naked down the street, and now they are commanding him to leave the hospital. If anyone tries to stop him, he will, he warns, kill them with his mental death ray. Smith is suffering from a psychotic break, and, so afflicted, he departs radically from ideal conditions of freedom. But Smith is still the same person as he was before his psychosis; indeed, imagine that Smith recovers. It is Smith that recovers; it is Smith that returns to his old job, and so on. So this departure from ideal conditions of freedom, while great, is not great enough to make Smith fail to count as the same person as the one who, for example, ran naked down the street. That was Smith. So how great a departure from the ideal conditions of freedom is needed before one ceases to be a person?

There is no need to give a precise answer to this question. Consider an analogy with restaurants. Where does one restaurant end and other begin? Suppose my favorite restaurant moves. Is it a new restaurant with the same name? Or suppose it changes owners and names but nothing else. Is it the same restaurant under a different name? Or suppose that in summer it serves food outside over a somewhat indeterminate area. Where does it begin and end? Suppose this outside area acquires its own chef, menu, and regular clientele. Are there really two restaurants under one name? It would be foolish to look for a precise, once-and-for-all answer to these questions because in many cases the answers may go either way; it is a matter of decision. Nonetheless, despite this sort of vagueness (if, indeed, it really is a species of vagueness), the concept of a restaurant is useful and, in fact, perfectly in order. This is true because, by and large in the typical cases, we have no trouble telling where one restaurant ends and another begins.

Similarly, in the case of the concept of a person, not giving a precise, once-and-for-all answer to the question "How far is too far?" does not mean that the concept is not perfectly in order. But there is a crucial difference between persons and restaurants. In the case of restaurants, the answer to the question "Is this the same restaurant?" could often be answered either way with equal validity. The answer is arbitrary, a matter of stipulation. However, as Bernard Williams has emphasized, the answer to the question "Is this the same person?" is rarely, if ever, a matter of stipulation.[12] So the question "How far is too far?" has to have a nonarbitrary answer. But this does not mean that the answer has to take the form of some single formula that covers all cases; what is required is that, by drawing on a variety of considerations—perhaps different considerations in different cases—we can give principled answers case by case.[13] I submit that a detailed examination of cases would

12. Bernard Williams, "The Self and the Future," in *Problems of the Self* (Cambridge: Cambridge University Press, 1974), pp. 61f.: "The bafflement seems, moreover to turn to plain absurdity if we move from conceptual undecidability to its close friend and neighbour, conventionalist decision." Nonetheless, I do not want to overemphasize the extent to which we are able to settle in a principled way questions about personal identity. I see no reason to deny that our notion of personal identity leaves certain questions of this sort undecided, that there are cases of "conceptual undecidability." Indeed, the account I have offered explains why there should be such cases since the notion of 'too far' may well have vague boundaries.

13. I should emphasize here that despite my remarks about 'too far', I do not agree with Derek Parfit's approach, which, as it were, fragments a person into a series of selves (see his "Personal Identity" in Perry, *Personal Identity*). Like Williams I want to "emphasize the basic importance for our thought of the ordinary idea of a self or person which undergoes changes of character, as opposed to an approach which, even if only metaphorically, would dissolve the person, under changes of character, into a series of 'selves' " (from Bernard Williams, "Persons, Character, and Morality," in *Moral Luck* [Cambridge: Cambridge University Press, 1981], p. 5). I think Williams's criticisms of Parfit are quite powerful, and as David Lewis has pointed out (David Lewis, "Survival and Identity," in Amelie Rorty, ed., *The Identities of Persons* [Berkeley: University of California Press, 1976]), the logical puzzles Parfit raises can be handled by tensed identity. Parfit's puzzles are of little significance for moral philosophy.

show that such principled answers are forthcoming and that our judgments about how far is too far coincide with our judgments about sameness of person.

The reply I have given to worries about how far is too far is the same sort of reply I would give to two other objections about vagueness in my analysis of personhood. The first objection concerns the notion of realizing self-concepts sufficiently often. I specified no minimal degree of "oftenness" that one must meet to count as a person. Second, in explaining the notion of commitment, I said that one regularly forms beliefs as to how to realize one's self-concepts sufficiently often. But I did not say how regularly was regularly. In response to both objections, I would argue that I do not need to give precise, once-and-for-all answers, for the same reasons that I do not need to in the case of "too far."

There are three additional reasons to accept the account of what it is to be a person.

1. The analysis illuminates the role that freedom plays in the concept of a person. I do not mean just the fact that the analysis makes the ability to act freely a necessary condition of being a person. What I have in mind is the intuition about persons expressed in Heidegger's cryptic formula: a person is "das Seiende, dem es in seinem Sein um dieses selbst geht."[14] Charles Taylor offers the following gloss; he suggests that the idea, at a first approximation, is that the "human subject is such that the question arises inescapably, which kind of being he is going to realize. A person is not just de facto a certain kind of being, with certain given desires, but it is somehow 'up to' him what kind of being he is going to be."[15] The idea that it is " 'up to' [one] what kind of being he is going to be" is a fundamentally important fact about persons. One reason is that we (typically) hold persons responsible for their characters (the kind of person they are, in one sense of 'kind of person'). Such ascriptions of responsibility would make little sense if one were "just de facto a kind of being with certain given desires." But this is not the only reason the point is important. The fact that we can shape ourselves is what gives our lives as persons their

14. Martin Heidegger, *Sein und Zeit*, 7th ed. (Tubingen: Niemayer Verlag, 1953), p. 42.
15. Charles Taylor, "Responsibility for Self," in Rorty, *The Identities of Persons*, pp. 281–282.

most interesting and most problematical aspects—as literature and
history so amply attest.

On the suggested account, a person is certainly not "just de facto
a certain kind of being with certain given desires." Insofar as a
person has the ability to act freely, he has the ability to eliminate
and create motives; furthermore, while to be a person is to realize
a certain self-concept-realizing order over time, which such order
the person realizes is 'up to' that person since the order is a product
of the person's exercising his ability to act freely. Consider Edwards
and Jones. Suppose Edwards's life divides into these periods of
maximal commitment: $T_{1,e}, \ldots, T_{n,e}$; Jones's into these: $T_{1,j}, \ldots, T_{n,j}$.
The T_e's and the T_j's need not have any periods of commitment in
common; the collections of expansive self-concepts to which Edwards is committed may be totally disjoint from those to which
Jones is committed. Moreover, even if the T_e's and the T_j's should
have periods in common, these periods need not occur in the same
order in Edwards's life as in Jones's life. The reason is that the
change from one T_e or T_j to another occurs under conditions that
do not depart too far from ideal conditions of freedom, and as such
it is a change that is, to some extent at least, under the direction
and control of the person involved. The particular pattern is 'up
to' the person. In general, there is no one fixed sequence of periods
of commitment such that every person passes through those periods
in that particular sequence.

2. The account explains an important Lockean intuition about
persons. Locke defines a person as "thinking intelligent being, that
has reason and reflection, and can consider itself as itself, the same
thinking thing in different times and places."[16] The idea here is
that a person is a being with certain mental capacities: memory,
self-consciousness, and reasoning. The analysis entails that one is
a person only if one has these capacities, and it also explains why
these capacities are important since they are necessary if one is to
achieve the self-imposed, self-concept-realizing order under conditions that do not depart too far from ideal conditions of freedom.

3. The third point concerns memory. It is clear that the analysis
makes memory essential to personal identity. Memory plays an
essential role in the generation of the self-imposed, self-concept-

16. Locke, *Essay*, II. 27, p. 2.

realizing order that obtains within any maximal period of commitment to realizing a collection of self-concepts, and a considerable degree of memory is required if conditions are not to depart too far from ideal condition of freedom.[17] But one might object here that the account does not explain the fact that, as many memory theorists have urged, a special sort of memory—experiential memory—is intimately involved in personal identity.

Richard Wollheim, for example, notes that

> there are different types of memory, and to claim that memory is criterial of personal identity on behalf of some types would be ridiculous, and therefore it is essential to get clear the type we are talking about. The relevant type of memory I call "experiential memory," and experiential memory can be distinguished from the irrelevant types by two differential features. The first feature is phenomenological and it is that, if I experientially remember an action or an experience, then I remember that action or experience from the inside. There is, critically, a point of view to the memory-experience. The second feature concerns the way an experiential memory is reported, and it is that, if I experientially remember, say, an action that I did or an experience that I suffered, then, if I report the memory (something that I might or might not do), I characteristically report it by saying "I remember doing, suffering, such-and-such" or "I remember my doing, my suffering, such-and-such"— all in contrast with "I remember that I did, that I suffered, such-and-such," which is more appropriate for the report of an external type of memory or one that does not contain a point of view.[18]

Now, in fact, the suggested account of personhood does provide a basis for explaining why experiential memory plays a crucial role in personal identity. To see this, we first need to note that although Wollheim's explanation is correct as far as it goes, it omits an essential epistemological feature of experiential memory. Suppose I seem to remember—seem to remember experientially—finger painting with yellow paint in kindergarten. The scene unfolds in my imagination, with me in the center of it making swirls of yellow

17. Some may think that I am open to the circularity objection often lodged against memory-theories of identity. The objection is that the analysis of memory must appeal to the concept of a person. However this claim about the analysis of memory is incorrect; see John Perry, "Personal Identity, Memory, and the Problem of Circularity," in Perry, *Personal Identity*.

18. Richard Wollheim, "On Persons and Their Lives," in Amelie Oksenberg Rorty, ed., *Explaining Emotions* (Berkeley: University of California Press, 1980), p. 406.

on a large piece of paper. Apart from this memory-experience I have no evidence that I finger-painted with yellow paint; I do not have the painting, nor do I still know anyone that saw me paint it. Even so, unless there is some reason to think that memory is deceiving me, I count as not just seeming to remember but as really remembering and hence as knowing that I finger-painted. A vast amount of what we take ourselves to know about our past is known on this sort of basis. In general, despite the fact that one can have delusive memory-experiences, we typically take cases of seeming to remember experientially as genuine cases and hence as yielding knowledge.[19]

To see the relevance of this epistemological feature to personal identity, recall that when one acts freely, the source of the action is "in" oneself, not "foreign." So, insofar as the ordered pattern of change and behavior associated with persons is imposed on one's life by exercising the ability to act freely, the source of that order is "in" oneself—the order is *self*-imposed. Memory plays an essential role in the generation of this order; since the relevant form of memory is experiential memory, this is consistent with the order having its source "in" oneself. To count as remembering, the mere memory-experience is, typically, sufficient. One needs only one's own experience; one need not rely on the testimony of others, for example, or on any other sort of "outside" source of evidence. If experiential memory did not have this epistemological status, it would be at best problematic to explain how the source of a free person's action truly lay "in" him.

A Role for the Body

But what of the intuition, noted at the beginning of the chapter, that the body plays an important role in personal identity? The account of personhood entails that a certain order in one's mental life is a necessary and sufficient condition of personal identity over time. The analysis assigns no role to the body.

Or so it seems. The analysis does not explicitly assign the body any role, but it does do so implicitly. The requirement that "throughout T conditions never depart too far from ideal conditions

---

19. I am only arguing that this is our attitude toward experiential memory; providing an adequate rationale for this attitude is a task of some difficulty.

of freedom" presupposes that one is able to remember a sufficient number of one's self-concept-realizing experiences. There are compelling arguments that the explanation of what it is for a mental state to count as a memory must treat such states as states of a body. Sydney Shoemaker, for example, argues as follows:

> In order to establish what the memories of other people are I have to be able to identify them in a bodily way. I cannot accept sentences offered by other people beginning with the words "I remember" quite uncritically. I must be assured first, that these utterances really are memory claims, that the speaker understands the meaning of the words he is using, and secondly, that his memory claims are reliable. . .it is essential, if either of these requirements is to be satisfied, for me to be able to identify the maker of the apparent memory claims in a independent bodily way. In order to be sure that his remarks really are intended as memory claims, I have to see that he generally uses the form of words in question in connection with antecedent states of affairs of which he has been a witness. And to do this I must be assured that he is at one time uttering a memory sentence and at another earlier time is witness of the event he purports to describe; in other words I must be able to identify him at different times without taking his apparent memories into account. The point is enforced by the second requirement about the conditions under which I can take his memory claims as trustworthy. To do this I must be able to establish at least that he was physically present at and, thus, in a position to observe the state of affairs he now claims to recollect.[20]

These considerations would seem to have considerable force. But what exactly do they show?

It might seem that they show that identification of Smith-today as the same person as Smith-yesterday requires that the body of Smith-today be the same body as the body of Smith-yesterday. But this is not correct. The most that these considerations show is that the body of Smith-today must stand in a relation R to the body of Smith-yesterday, where standing in relation R is sufficient to secure that events witnessed by Smith-yesterday are events that Smith-

20. Shoemaker argues this way in Sydney S. Shoemaker, "Personal Identity and Memory," *Journal of Philosophy*, 56, no. 22 (October 22, 1959), 868. The quoted passage is from Anthony Quinton's summary of Shoemaker's position in Quinton's "The Soul," in Perry, *Personal Identity*. I agree with Quinton that "it is only the necessity of local bodily continuity that is established, not the necessary association of a person with one particular body for the whole duration of either" (p. 70).

today can remember. Of course, one may find it difficult to see what R could be if it is not just sameness of body, but there are examples that suggest that one and the same person can have different bodies at different times.

Thus Smith and Jones step into the matter-transmitter to travel together to a distant planet. Something goes wrong enroute, however, and while two intact bodies step out at the other end, the Smith-body has all of Jones's memories, character traits, patterns of emotion reaction, personal loyalties, plans, projects, desires, hopes, fears, beliefs, and so on. The same is true in reverse for the Jones-body and Smith. It would seem that the person whose body was the Jones-body before transmission is the same person as the person whose body is the Smith-body after transmission and vice versa for the person whose body was the Smith-body before transmission. At least, it seems so to those who share a certain intuition about personal identity. David Lewis has expressed the intuition forcefully:

> What is it that matters in survival? Suppose I wonder whether I will survive the coming battle, brainwashing, brain transplant, journey by matter-transmitter, purported reincarnation or resurrection, fission into twins, fusion with someone else, or what not. What do I really care about? . . .
>
> I answer, along with many others: *what matters in survival is mental continuity and connectedness.* When I consider various cases in between commonplace survival and commonplace death, I find that what I mostly want in wanting survival is that my mental life should flow on. My present experiences, thoughts beliefs, desires, and traits of character should have appropriate future successors. My total present mental state should be but one momentary stage in a succession mental states. These successive states should be interconnected in two ways. First, by bonds of similarity. Change should be gradual rather than sudden, and (at least in some respects) there should not be too much change overall. Second, by bonds of lawful causal dependence. Such change as there is should conform, for the most part, to lawful regularities concerning the succession of mental states—regularities, moreover, that are exemplified in everyday cases of survival. And this should not be so by accident . . . but rather because each succeeding mental state causally depends for its character on the the states immediately before it.[21]

21. Lewis, "Survival and Identity," p. 17. Lewis is primarily concerned with certain logical difficulties. I agree with him that the solution of these difficulties lies in an appeal to tensed identity.

In the matter-transmitter example, Jones's (Smith's) "mental life flows on," although it does so—it would seem—in the Smith-body (Jones-body). So is the person whose body was the Jones-body (Smith-body) before transmission the same person as the person whose body is the Smith-body (Jones-body) after transmission?

Many do not find the answer to be a clear yes. The suggested analysis of personhood explains why. According to the analysis, one is a person only if during the time in which one exists "conditions never depart too far from ideal conditions of freedom." In the matter-transmitter example and similar examples, do conditions depart too far from ideal conditions of freedom? In part, this is a question of whether there is a relation R between the Jones-body (Smith-body) before transmission and the Smith-body (Jones-body) after transmission such that standing in the relation R is sufficient to secure that events witnessed before transmission by the person in the Jones-body (Smith-body) can be remembered after transmission by the person in the Smith-body (Jones-body). I think there is such a relation R, but it is not obvious that there is. It is a question of what is required for the preservation of memory, and this is certainly not obvious before philosophical analysis and perhaps scientific investigation. It is a virtue of the account of personhood that this question is left undecided in the appeal to conditions that do not depart "too far from ideal conditions of freedom."

A Final Point

Some may find that since I have frequently described people as motivated by beliefs as to how to realize self-concepts, the examples given in this chapter (as well as in the previous one) represent people as peculiarly selfish. I have focused exclusively on this sort of motivation because it is the sort relevant to the issues I am discussing; however, nothing I have said entails (and indeed I do not think) that all motivation that arises out of conceptions arises out of self-conceptions. Moreover, there is nothing necessarily selfish about motivation supplied by self-concepts. Suppose that one reason I oppose child pornography is that I am committed to the self-concept *respecting human dignity*, and I believe child pornography degrades human dignity. There is nothing essentially selfish about my motivation. I am acting out of a concern for others—a concern so deeply held that it finds expression in my very identity as person, manifesting itself in a commitment to realizing a self-concept.

This completes the discussion of personhood. The next topic is enjoyment.

4 Enjoyment

The concept of enjoyment is of considerable interest in its own right, apart from its role in the account of happiness, for it is a focal point at which diverse conceptual themes intersect. To take two especially relevant examples, consider the concepts of motivation and of justification for action. The most obvious connection is that the prospect of enjoyment is frequently a motivation to, and a justification for, action. A less obvious connection is mediated by the concept of desiring something for its own sake; on the one hand, there are important connections between that concept and the concepts of motivation and of reasons for action, and on the other hand, desiring a thing for its own sake is, as I shall argue, a necessary condition of enjoying that thing. So what is enjoyment?

Enjoyment and Desire

I will define enjoyment by completing the following biconditional:

$$x \text{ enjoys } \varphi \text{ at } t \text{ if and only if} \ldots,$$

where φ is an experience or an activity of x. I am understanding the verb 'enjoys' in such a way that $\ulcorner x$ enjoys φ at $t \urcorner$ implies $\ulcorner x \, \varphi s$ at $t \urcorner$. Thus $\ulcorner x$ enjoys φ at $t \urcorner$ is to be understood as equivalent

119

to $\ulcorner$x is enjoying φ at t $\urcorner$. So why not use the latter form and avoid this special stipulation about the verb 'enjoys'? Simply because a constant use of 'is enjoying' leads to awkward and stilted expressions. Another preliminary point concerns the restriction of values of 'φ' to experiences and activities. This restriction may at first sight seem questionable: I can enjoy a meal or a painting, neither of which is an experience or an activity. But I can enjoy the meal only if I eat it; the painting, only if I look at it. In general, where y is something other than an experience or activity, x enjoys y if and only if x enjoys φ, where φ is a suitable experience or activity involving y. Consequently, the restriction on values of 'φ' involves no irrecoverable loss of generality. But more importantly, if we were to examine explanations of the form 'because he or she enjoys it', we would find that what is enjoyed is always either explicitly or implicitly understood to be an experience or an activity, and it this primacy in explanation that motivates restricting values of 'φ' to experiences and activities; as the explanations we advance show, we treat as derivative the enjoyment of things other than experiences and activities.[1]

The first step toward defining enjoyment is to note the connection between enjoyment and desire, and I should remark that, in the discussion that follows, I will not distinguish between S-desires and E-desires; everything will apply equally to both forms of desire. The most basic point is that you enjoy φ at a time t only if you desire at t to (have or do) φ. The temporal qualification "at t" is necessary since the desire to φ need not exist prior to enjoying φ. Suppose, for example, that you find yourself cornered by a talkative stranger with whom you have no initial desire to converse, but you begin to enjoy talking with him. As long as you enjoy doing so, you want to do so; you may, however, form this desire at the same time that you begin to enjoy the conversation.[2]

1. As David Hills has pointed out to me, my use of the words 'experience' and 'activity' can be easily misunderstood if those words are interpreted in the light of philosophical traditions that have exploited the words; so I should stress that I regard the proper philosophical understanding of these words as an open question.

2. As this example illustrates, I can desire to φ during an interval of time t even when I am, and know I am, φing throughout t. This will seem counterintuitive to those who see desire as related to a "perceived lack," but it should cause no problems to those who think of desires as states that move us to action. See, for example, Brian O'Shaughnessy, *The Will* (Cambridge: Cambridge University Press, 1980), 2,

We can motivate the claim that desiring to φ is a necessary condition of enjoying φ by considering a class of examples in which it evidently follows from one's not desiring to φ that one is not enjoying φ.[3] Suppose I claim that you are enjoying listening to an indifferently performed piano piece. It certainly seems clear that you can refute this claim by establishing that you have no desire to listen to the music. You may respond to my claim by pointing out that you are in fact trying to enjoy it (it is the performance of a friend and you want to be able to say sincerely that you enjoyed it); however, the indifferent performance leaves you indifferent—neither desiring to listen nor desiring not to listen (what motivates you to sit there and try to enjoy the music is the desire not to disappoint your friend; unfortunately, since you lack the desire to listen, your mind keeps wandering). The complete absence of any desire to listen to the music certainly seems sufficient to refute my claim that you are enjoying listening to it. There are any number of similar examples we could consider to reinforce this point; how-

---

p. 295f.: "A brief word on desire. When action occurs, it is in the final analysis this phenomenon that underlies all of the workings of the act generative mental machinery." Thus desire is what explains my acting so as to maintain *ongoing* experiences and activities whose occurrence I want, even when I know such experiences are occurring (compare quotes from Hobbes below). O'Shaughnessy characterizes desire as a "striving towards an act of fulfillment" (2, p. 296). In this, he agrees with Aristotle; the root meaning of Aristotle's most general word for desire—'orexis'—is "a reaching out after." Plato is one source of the "perceived lack" view (see the *Symposium*, for example). This view is indefensible as a general characterization of desire. The problem is revealed by Hobbes. In the *Leviathan*, Hobbes characterizes desire as an "endeavour ... toward something which causes it," but he restricts the use of 'desire' to cases in which the object of desire is absent. However, he then notes: "that which men desire, they are also said to LOVE: and to HATE those things for which they have aversion. So that desire and love are the same thing; save that by desire, we always signify the absence of the object; by love most commonly the presence of the same. So also by aversion we signify the absence; and by hate, the presence of the object" (Thomas Hobbes, *Leviathan*, in *The English Works of Thomas Hobbes*, ed. Sir William Molesworth [London: John Bohn, 1939]). Surely, Hobbes is right. If desire requires the absence of the object, we need a word for that attitude that is just like desire except that its object is present—the attitude that explains why one would resist removal of the object. Remove the object and this attitude *is* 'desire'. But then why not just say that 'love' and 'desire' are just the same state—whether the object is present or absent? Or at least say that 'love' and 'desire' are instances of some single generic desire-state? As Hobbes says, "love and desire are the same thing."

3. The claim that desiring to φ is a necessary condition of enjoying φ is common. For a recent example, see Richard Brandt, *A Theory of the Good and the Right* (Oxford: Clarendon Press, 1979).

ever, it will be more convincing to turn our attention to a class of prima facie counterexamples in which a person purportedly enjoys φ, although he finds φing wholly distasteful or disagreeable.

Suppose that Smith is roundly condemning the party from which he has just returned after staying only a short while. The main theme running through his complaints is that he wanted nothing the party had to offer. He finally mitigates these complaints, however, by confessing that the party was not completely wretched and that he actually enjoyed it a little. If this confession is consistent with Smith's claim that he wanted nothing the party had to offer, we have described a case in which a person enjoys φ at t without at t desiring to φ.

But why should we grant that the confession and the claim are consistent? After all, Smith has roundly condemned the party, insisting that he wanted nothing it had to offer; if we really take Smith seriously about this, it is difficult to understand how he could have enjoyed this party. Suppose we ask Smith what it was that he enjoyed about the party. He might refuse to answer this question, for he might insist that he just enjoyed attending the party without enjoying any particular aspect of it. For the moment, however, suppose that Smith says that he enjoyed dancing and that he also insists that he did not want to dance. This does not simply mean that he did not want to dance *prior* to dancing. It means that throughout the time he was purportedly enjoying dancing, he simply did not desire to dance.

Here the point made in the indifferently performed music example applies with considerable force. In that example, the absence of a desire to listen to the music certainly seemed sufficient to refute the claim that you enjoyed listening to the music; likewise here, the complete lack of desire to dance seems sufficient to establish that Smith did not enjoy dancing, for given that he completely lacks any desire to dance, must we not count him as completely indifferent to dancing or, if he wants not to dance, as wholly disinclined to dance? Neither of these characterizations is consistent with a description of Smith as enjoying dancing.

Essentially, these same considerations would apply if Smith said that what he enjoyed was not dancing but talking with friends, or listening to music, or watching the people, or whatever. In fact, it is difficult to see how Smith can provide any convincing answer to the question of what it was about the party that he enjoyed. But as we already noted, Smith may reject the question and insist that although he neither desired nor enjoyed any particular thing the party had to offer, he nonetheless enjoyed attending it. Suppose that this is what he replies and that he also insists that, even though he enjoyed attending the party, he did not want to be there at all.

Is this sufficient to cast doubt on the claim that desiring to φ is a necessary condition of enjoying φ? I do not think so, for we surely must reject Smith's claim that he enjoyed the party. We could do so simply by another appeal to the point made in the indifferently performed music example. But there is also a more direct reply available; Smith at no time desires to attend the party and does not have any desire for anything the party has to offer—dancing, music, conversations with friends, or anything else; as we have just seen, he cannot have enjoyed any of these things. This is a crystal clear example of not enjoying a party.

This is sufficient to show that the counterexample (and others like it) is not successful. Of course, some may still be skeptical of the claim that desiring φ is a necessary condition of enjoying φ. One way to meet such skepticism is to develop the definition and demonstrate its success as a basis for clarification and explanation. So let us assume the necessity of the condition and turn to the further task of definition.

Given our assumption about the connection between enjoyment and desire, the simplest definition of enjoyment would equate enjoyment with the satisfaction of desire: x enjoys φ if and only if φs and x desires to φ. But this fails since there are many cases in which we satisfy our desires without any accompanying enjoyment. You may satisfy your desire to go to the dentist without experiencing enjoyment. Dental treatment may be an ordeal of discomfort and anxiety to which you submit only because it is a means to the end of dental health.

Reflection on the dentist example suggests that we can make progress toward a definition by distinguishing between desiring something for its own sake and desiring something only as a means to an end. In the dentist example, you want to go to the dentist only because it is a means to the end of dental health, and the fact is certainly one you could cite to refute the claim that you enjoyed going. This argues strongly for taking desiring to φ for its own sake as a necessary condition for enjoying φ. Considerations of simplicity argue for taking this necessary condition to be sufficient as well: that is, x enjoys φ if and only if x φs and x desires to φ for its own sake. However, as it stands, this suggestion is false. Consider the following example.

You have never been deep-sea fishing, but you desire to go for its own sake. Still, it may happen that you fail to experience enjoyment when you satisfy this desire. We can imagine, in fact, that you find the entire experience of deep-sea fishing distasteful. You get seasick; you are disgusted by the crowded, noisy deck from which you must fish; you are repelled by the necessity of bare-handedly catching the small, live fish used for bait, and you are even more repelled by the fact that, once you have succeeded in grabbing the bait, you have to impale it by the gills on your hook. But your desire to fish survives the initial shock of these experiences, and so you continue to fish even though you admit to yourself that you are not enjoying it. In fact, you continue to fish only because you hope that you *will* enjoy it. At the moment, however, your desire to fish is waning. It persists, but it persists despite your experiences; only the hope that things will change keeps it alive.

This is enough to show that enjoyment cannot be defined as satisfying a desire for something for its own sake. You desire to go deep-sea fishing for its own sake, but engaging in that activity, even while you have the desire to do so, does not lead to enjoyment. So we are back to regarding desiring φ for its own sake as a necessary but not sufficient condition of enjoying φ. What do we need to add to get a sufficient condition?

We can answer by considering the following continuation of the deep-sea-fishing case. A large fish suddenly strikes your line, and all of your attention is immediately focused on the fight to land it. Your seasick feeling, your impinging awareness of the crowded deck, and your qualms about catching the live bait are instantly eclipsed by the excitement of the fight; moreover, after you have landed the fish, you find that you are no longer seasick. The deck no longer seems inhospitably crowded but full of cooperative people who are congratulating you on your catch. Even catching and hooking the live bait now seems to be just one of those necessities that disquiet only the uninitiated. You find now that you want to fish not in spite of, but because of, your experiences. You are—as you now realize—enjoying it.

So the activity of deep-sea fishing has been transformed from one you did not enjoy to one you do. The crucial question is: how are we to characterize this transformation? Answering this question will enable us to formulate an adequate definition of enjoyment.

A Definition of Enjoyment

My view is that the transformation consists in certain changes in your beliefs and desires. There are two basic points to note. First, it is clear that one fundamental aspect of the transformation is the change that takes place in the way you conceive of your activity of deep-sea fishing. You come to think of that activity differently. The deck, for example, is no longer crowded; rather, it is full of cooperative people. Catching the live bait is no longer repulsive but merely a necessity that no longer has any power to upset you now that you count yourself among the initiated. And so on.

To understand this change, consider that your activity of deep-sea fishing is an individual, nonrepeatable event. Deep-sea fishing is a repeatable event, and so is your deep-sea fishing, since you may go again and again. But each time you go, your activity of deep-sea fishing at that time is a particular, nonrepeatable individual. As you fish you are exposed to the entire temporal span of this individual. Consequently, your knowledge about it becomes more and more complete as the activity progresses; or, as we can put it, you acquire an increasingly detailed and complete array of concepts, which you believe that the activity realizes. For example, you believe that the confident way in which you now grab the live bait realizes the concept *being one of the initiated*, and you believe that your activity of deep-sea fishing realizes the concept *doing something exciting*. Moreover, that activity is what causes you to acquire this ever-increasing array of concepts. This last observation is essential to an adequate understanding of enjoyment, for the principal idea behind the final definition of enjoyment is that enjoyment consists in a certain harmony between three elements: the activity or experience, the concepts that the experience or activity causes one to believe it realizes, and a certain desire in which these same concepts figure.

The second of the two basic points about the deep-sea-fishing example concerns the change in your array of concepts, which cannot itself explain why you suddenly enjoy deep-sea fishing. Even with this changed conception, you might still have found deep-sea fishing unenjoyable; you might simply have been indifferent to it. Such a response would have been quite compatible with your changed conception. What happens in the actual example, however, is that, in addition to the change in your conception, there is a change in your desires about your activity of deep-sea fishing. I emphasized this point in presenting the example when I described you as wanting to fish "not in spite of, but because of, your experiences." But what exactly does this change in your desires consist of?

To answer this question, let t be the time at which the change occurs, and let C be the array of concepts that your deep-sea fishing causes you at t to believe are realized by that activity.[4] The essential point is that although the change in your conception does not itself explain why you suddenly enjoy deep-sea fishing, you could use these concepts to indicate the features that make your deep-sea fishing something you desire not in spite of, but because of, your experiences; certainly, the features picked out by these concepts are the key to explaining this change in your desire. Indeed, we can describe the change in your desires by saying that you form a *new* desire to engage in your activity of deep-sea fishing, a desire that—in a way I explain below—involves the array of concepts C. It is the fact that the desire involves the concepts in C that makes it new at t, for it is a desire that you would have had prior to t only if you had conceived of your activity of deep-sea fishing and falling under the concepts in C, and you did not so conceive of that activity prior to t.

More precisely, what I am suggesting is that at t you come to *desire, of your activity of deep-sea fishing, under the concepts in C, that it occur.* The formulation of the suggestion needs clarification: what is the force of the expression 'of your activity of deep-

4. Strictly speaking, we do not need to suppose that C is the total array you acquire at t; C may be only a part of it.

sea fishing, under the concepts of C'? There is a technical motivation behind using this expression; when I generalize from the deep-sea-fishing example to the definition of enjoyment, I will rewrite this expression as 'of the experience or activity φ, under the concept in C', where 'φ' and 'C' are variables bound by quantifiers. This provides a clear and unproblematic representation of what gets quantified where. We will be combining quantifiers with the verbs 'believes,' and 'desires'; it is well known that such quantification can lead to problems unless care is taken. So I am adopting the usual Quinean convention that a singular term t' may be substituted *salva veritate* for a term t occurring in the context $\ulcorner\ldots$ desires (or believes), of t, that $\ldots\urcorner$—given the true identity $\ulcorner t = t'\urcorner$.[5]

So much for motivation. We still need to know what it means to describe you as desiring, of your deep-sea fishing, under the concepts in C, that you should engage in that activity. We can answer this question by presenting an example in which such a description has a clear sense and then by explaining why we should handle the deep-sea fishing example in the same way. Suppose that I find you placing a bet on a fifty-to-one shot; you remark, "I want to bet on the long shot." In saying this you do two things by the phrase 'bet on the long shot'. First, you identify the activity—betting on the long shot—in which you want to engage, so it is certainly true to say that you desire, of your activity of placing the bet, that it occur. Second—and this is the essential point—by 'bet on the long shot', you express a concept—*betting on a long shot*—which you take your activity of placing the bet to realize. It is the realization of this concept that recommends that activity to you as desirable. We can express this involvement of the concept *betting on a long shot* in your desire by saying that you desire of your activity of placing the bet, under the concept *betting on a long shot*, that it occur. This is to be understood in such a way that, to satisfy this desire, not only must you bet on the horse, but that activity must realize the concept *betting on a long shot*. Part of what you want after all is to bet on a *long shot*. In general, one's φing satisfies one's

5. W. V. Quine, "Quantifiers and Propositional Attitudes," in *Ways of Paradox* (Cambridge: Harvard University Press, 1976), pp. 185–196; see especially pp. 188–191.

desire, of the experience or activity φ, under the concept c, that it occur only if φ realizes c.

There is a clear analogy between the long-shot example and the deep-sea-fishing example, for in the latter example the concepts in C play a role exactly analogous to the role of the concept *betting on a long shot.* This is the point we made above when we emphasized the fact that you could use the concepts in C to indicate certain features that your deep-sea fishing exhibits at t—those features being the ones that make your deep-sea fishing something you desire "not in spite of, but because of, your experiences." You could point out that the deck seems to be full of cooperative and friendly people, that you are being congratulated on your catch, that you are no longer seasick, and so on. Thus it is reasonable to suggest that what happens at t is that you form a new desire involving the concepts in C; that is, you come to desire, of your deep-sea fishing, under the concepts in C, that it occur.

Why should we accept the suggestion that you form precisely this desire? Because it is part of the best description and explanation of the change that we initially described as your coming to want to fish "not in spite of but because of your experiences," for accepting the suggestion allows us to explain why you begin to enjoy your activity of deep-sea fishing. The explanation rests on two points. The first is that your activity of deep-sea fishing causes you at t to desire, of that activity, under the concepts in C, that it occur. To see this, consider that your activity of deep-sea fishing plays a central role in the causal ancestry of your acquiring the array of concepts C. Consequently, it also plays a central role in the causal ancestry of your forming the desire in question.

The second point is that your activity not only causes but also satisfies this desire. Consider: you are engaging in this activity, you believe that the concepts in C apply to it, and you desire to engage in the activity so conceived. Therefore, your desire is satisfied. Or, as we should say, you *experience* the satisfaction of your desire,— since, as we are understanding 'desire under a concept', actual satisfaction requires the *truth* of your belief that the concepts in C apply to the activity. I am understanding 'experience' as creating an intentional context so the 'you experience the satisfaction of your desire' does not imply 'your desire is satisified'. The concept of *experience* that I am invoking needs more explaination than this, but let me postpone that discussion.

The point to emphasize now is that your activity causes a desire and simultaneously ensures that you will experience its satisfaction. I suggest that it is exactly this sort of link between causation and satisfaction that typifies enjoyment: for you to enjoy your activity of deep-sea fishing *just is* for that activity to exhibit this sort of link between causation and satisfaction. More fully, enjoyment consists in a kind of harmony between three elements: your activity of deep-sea fishing, your belief that this activity falls under the concepts in C, and your desire to engage in that activity so conceived. The harmony between these elements consists in the fact that, in causing this belief and this desire, your activity of deep-sea fishing ensures that you will experience the satisfaction of the desire it causes. Given the belief and the desire your activity produces, you *must* experience the satisfaction of that desire. This harmony between causation and satisfaction is enjoyment. Thus in the deep-sea-fishing case, we can see why you begin to enjoy deep-sea fishing once you begin to desire, of your activity, under the concepts in C, that you should engage in that activity.

Generalizing from the deep-sea-fishing example, we obtain the following definition of enjoyment.[6] To formulate the definition, let t' be a moment of time slightly prior to t;[7] we can say that x enjoys an experience or activity φ at t if and only if there is a collection of concepts C such that:

first, x φs at t'.

second, x's φing causes x at t

  (a) to believe that φ realizes the concepts in C;

  (b) to desire, of φ, under C, that it occur for its own sake.

Two comments to the second condition are in order. I should clarify an ambiguity in the expression used in (a): "believe that φ

6. The definition I will give has affinities with Kant's definition of enjoyment in the third *Critique*: "The consciousness of the causality of a representation in respect of the state of the Subject as one tending to *preserve a continuance* of that state, may be here said to denote in a general way what is called pleasure." *Critique of Judgement*, trans. J. C. Meredith (Oxford: Oxford University Press, 1952), Part I, p. 61.

7. My treatment of the relation between enjoyment and time is artificial; the point is to accommodate an insistence that causes must precede effects. A more realistic way to handle time would be to take t to be a suitably short interval of time—cause and effect occurring in this interval. I have avoided this because it is more complicated and because the artificiality of the treatment in the text is harmless.

realizes the concepts in C." Consider this instance of the expression: "Jones believes that his activity of deep-sea fishing realizes the concept *doing something exciting*." This sentence may be read as attributing to Jones the belief he could express by stating, "My activity of deep-sea fishing realizes the concept *doing something exciting*." Or it may be read as attributing to Jones the belief he could express by saying, "My deep-sea fishing is exciting." In the former sentence there is an explicit reference to the concept *doing something exciting*, a reference that is absent from the latter. It is the second reading we want; that is, "Jones believes that his activity of deep-sea fishing realizes the concept *doing something exciting*" is to be true just in case Jones believes that his deep-sea fishing is exciting. The same is true for all other instances of "believe that φ realizes the concepts in C." One motive for this stipulation is to allow lower animals to satisfy (a), for, while I take it that some lower animals can have beliefs, I also take it that they cannot have beliefs that are explicitly about concepts. Worries about lower animals may also arise over the use in (b) of the notion of a desire under a concept, and I take up this issue later.

The second comment is that (b) reads "to desire, of φ, under the concepts in C, that it occur," not "that it continue." Although the latter reading sounds more natural to many, it leads to an incorrect account of enjoyment. Suppose I enjoy writing the last word of an essay. It would be implausible to suggest that I desire to continue to write the last word. What would this mean? I certainly don't desire to write the word over and over again; nor do I desire to draw out the activity of writing the last word for as long as possible since I can enjoy writing the last word even if I scribble it down hurriedly. Rather, what I desire is that my writing down the last word should occur.[8]

Now let us turn to objections; there are two that require consideration.

8. Compare J. C. B. Gosling, *Pleasure and Desire* (Oxford: Oxford University Press, 1979), p. 65. Gosling's example is of enjoying breaking the good news. His discussion of pleasure contains a number of interesting examples. He deploys many of his examples against accounts of enjoyment that assert one or another link between enjoyment and desire. I think my analysis is actually supported, not refuted, by Gosling's examples as the analysis explains, or explains away, the apparent counterexamples.

Two Objections

First objection.   The first objection is that the way I have defined enjoyment ignores the evident fact that there is *something it
is like* to enjoy an experience or an activity, that there is a distinctive
experiential quality associated with enjoyment. The claim is that I
have ignored this fact since all that I require for enjoyment is an appropriate belief and desire, and it would seem that one can have
such a belief and desire without experiencing any special felt
quality.

The first point to note in reply is that enjoyments will exhibit an
experiential quality if the belief involved is an *occurrent* belief and
the desire a *felt* desire. An experiential quality may, in this way,
be involved in enjoyment, but must it be? My answer—with qualifications—is yes: the distinctive experiential quality of enjoyment
consists in having a felt desire to φ at precisely the same time that
one occurrently believes that one is φing. At one at the same time,
one both feels desire and has it before one's mind that this very
desire is satisfied.

One advantage of this suggestion is that it allows me to explain
what I mean by the expression 'experience the satisfaction of one's
desire': namely, having—at one and the same time—the felt desire
to φ and the occurrent belief that one is φing. Given this understanding of the expression, it is clear for example, that "I experience
the satisfaction of my desire to look at the Cézannes" does not imply
"My desire is satisfied" (since my belief that I am looking at Cézannes may be false). It also follows—by definition—that if one has
the felt desire to and the occurrent belief that one is φing, one *must*
experience the satisfaction of one's desire.

However, there would appear to be a serious difficulty. Imagine
yourself absorbed in deep-sea fishing. Your attention is fully focused on reeling in a large fish. You are enjoying deep-sea fishing,
but you do not occurrently believe that you are engaged in that
activity; that belief is not before your mind in the relevant way.
Moreover, although you desire to be deep-sea fishing, that desire is
not manifesting itself to you with a felt quality as you reel in the fish.

To see that this is not really a difficulty, suppose that, after land-
ing the fish, you stand back and survey the scene of your recent

efforts. You now have the felt desire to engage in deep-sea fishing, and as you feel this desire, you occurrently believe that you are now deep-sea fishing. As you continue to fish, this occurrent belief/felt desire pair is immediately at hand; that is, under suitable conditions, you would have the occurrent belief and the felt desire. The essential point is that if this belief/desire pair were not at hand, you would not count as enjoying deep-sea fishing. To see this, suppose that, in the deep sea fishing example, you never have a felt desire to engage in deep-sea fishing; you never feel this desire— no matter how carefully you reflect and introspect. When you stand back and survey the scene on the boat, you have—let us suppose— a sense of well-being but never the felt desire to fish. In such a case, you may be enjoying something—perhaps being on the boat, being in the open air; but you are not enjoying deep-sea fishing specifically, for—and I take this to be clear—*the object of enjoyment is the object of felt desire.* What gives enjoyment its special experiential character is having the felt desire simultaneously with the relevant occurrent belief.

In light of these considerations, the best course is to interpret 'believe' and 'desire' in the analysis of enjoyment to mean occurrent belief and felt desire. We can count the cases of enjoyment not involving such a occurrent belief/felt desire pair—but in which such a belief/desire pair is at hand—as secondary and derivative examples of enjoyment. These cases count as cases of enjoyment precisely because, given suitable circumstances, the primary phenomenon that is defined in terms of occurrent belief and felt desire would occur.

The second objection.   The second objection is that the definition cannot be correct since it cannot always be true that one enjoys φ only if (one's having or doing) φ causes one to have the required belief and desire. What of cases in which, before φing, one already believes the concepts in the array C apply to φ or one already desires, of φ, under C, that it occur? The objection is that one's φing cannot cause a belief or desire that already exists.

This objection rests on a confusion between *causing* and *bringing into existence.* Consider another example. The girders that support a bridge at a given moment certainly cause it to stand at the moment, even though it was already standing at the immediately preceding moment, so the girders could not cause the bridge to stand in the sense that they make it change from a nonstanding to a standing condition. The girders cause the bridge to stand in the sense that they causally *sustain* it in a standing condition. Similarly, an enjoyed experience or activity may causally sustain a preexisting belief or desire.

This answers the objection, but it does not leave us in a fully satisfactory position with regard to the causal requirement. What is the rationale for that requirement? I have yet to provide one.[9]

The first step toward providing the rationale is to note that to enjoy an experience or an activity is to respond to it in a certain way. The causal requirement is intended to capture this idea, for the causal requirement entails that an enjoyed experience or activity is one that exerts a certain power over the enjoyer. It makes one have a felt desire for its occurrence for its own sake; in addition, the experience or activity has the power to bring it before one's mind that it conforms to the concepts under which it is desired: it makes one

9. It may seem that I am ignoring obvious counterexamples to the causal requirement. Consider a varient of the deep-sea-fishing example. You have never been deep-sea fishing but you desire to go. The cause of this desire is the attractive picture of that activity that you have built up in your imagination. However, when you actually go, the activity does not—according to the objection we are now formulating—cause you to desire, of that activity, under an appropriate array of concepts, that it occur. You do nonetheless have this desire. You have it because, before ever going fishing, you already desired that *some* activity of deep-sea fishing occur; this is the desire caused by your imaginative picture. This desire is not a desire for the particular deep-sea-fishing activity in which you are now engaged. The desire caused by your imagined picture is not focused on any particular activity; it was simply a desire for *some* such activity. But when you combined this desire for some such activity with your belief that this particular activity is of the relevant sort, you form a desire, of *that particular activity*, under an appropriate array of concepts, that it occur. So you are deep-sea fishing; you believe that a certain array of concepts applies to that activity; and you desire, of that activity, under those concepts, that it occur (for its own sake). Consequently, you experience the satisfaction of this desire. Why isn't this enough for enjoyment?

The answer is that this is not a case in which the causal requirements fail to be fulfilled. Consider your belief that the relevant concepts apply to this particular activity of deep-sea fishing. This belief is caused by your activity of deep-sea fishing; the perception of that activity is an essential part of the causal ancestry of the belief that that activity satisfies certain concepts. But it is this belief and the desire that some activity of deep-sea fishing occur, that serve as the structured desire, of that particular activity, that *it* occur. So the activity is part of the causal ancestry of that structured desire.

occurrently believe that it realizes those concepts. The following example confirms that enjoyment involves such a response.

Jones is listening to a jazz band; he does not know the first thing about what makes jazz good, and so, as he listens to the music, he is unable to identify any feature that makes it good. Nonetheless, he desires, of the experience, under the concept *listening to good jazz*, that it occur for its own sake, and he believes that the experience realizes this concept. If one were to ask Jones why he was at the Blue Lagoon Jazz Club he would say that he believes that the music is good and wants to listen to it. Moreover, the experience of listening causes this desire and belief. If Jones were not listening to the music, he would not desire, of *that particular* experience, under the concept *listening to good jazz*, that it occur; nor would he believe, of *that particular* experience, that it realized the concept. But: the experience does not cause Jones to have a *felt* desire or an *occurrent* belief. As Jones sits at his table, his attention wanders. He looks at the people, listens to the background noise, wonders whether he should drink a different kind of scotch, worries about the fact that he forgot to pay the phone bill, and so on. Occasionally, the thought crosses his mind that the band is good. He thinks it must be good since it is playing at the Blue Lagoon, and this thought leads him to have a felt desire to listen to the music and the occurrent belief that he is listening to good jazz. But Jones cannot hear in the music any feature that makes it good; all jazz—good or bad—sounds more or less the same to him. And, because he actually finds all jazz rather uninteresting, the music fails to hold his attention; his mind wanders again, and the felt quality of the desire and the occurrentness of the belief fade away.

Jones does not respond to the music in the way required to count as enjoying it. If he were enjoying it, his attention would not wander in the way that it does. Indeed, this is just the sort of case in which we would say that Jones does not know enough about jazz to be able to enjoy it. At best, he is playing at enjoying the music. He may really enjoy being at the bar, or drinking, or watching the people, but listening to good jazz cannot be a true description of what he enjoys.

The causal requirement provides an explanation of why Jones does not count as enjoying the music. The experience of listening to the music does not cause a felt desire and an occurrent belief.

When Jones does have such a desire and belief, their source is his inference that the band must be good since it is playing at the Blue Lagoon; the source is not the experience itself. Someone who knows jazz might identify in the music the features that make it good, and in this way his experience of listening to the music might cause the relevant felt desire and occurrent belief; but since he is ignorant of what makes jazz good, this cannot happen in Jones's case.

Some may object that I am individuating causes too finely in distinguishing between the cause of a desire or a belief and the cause of the desire's being felt and the belief's being occurrent. After all, since the experience of listening to the music causes the desire, surely the experience must count as part of the causal ancestry of the desire's being felt, for the existence of the desire is a precondition of the desire's being felt. Likewise, *mutatis mutandis*, for the belief.

But this is not correct; that is, there is a way of understanding 'cause'—a common and ordinary way—and on that understanding, the above claims about causation are incorrect. This way of understanding 'cause' incorporates a distinction between preconditions and causes. Thus a precondition of a bridge's collapsing is that it be built, but, on the understanding of 'cause' I have in mind, the building of the bridge is not a cause of its collapsing. Of course, if we think of one total momentary state of the universe as the cause of the next total momentary state, the building of the bridge is a component of the cause of the bridge's collapsing (given that causation is a transitive relation). But this is not how I am understanding 'cause' here.

As I am understanding 'cause', we can distinguish between, for example, the cause of my saying "Hello" when I answer the phone— that cause being the ringing of the phone, my desire to answer, and so on—and the cause of my saying "Hello" loudly, which is caused by my extreme nervousness. I do not desire to say "Hello" loudly; it just happens.[10] My saying "Hello" is, of course, a precondition

10. The example is from Alvin Goldman, *A Theory of Human Action* (Englewood Cliffs, N.J.: Prentice-Hall, 1970), p. 3. Goldman is arguing against Donald Davidson's account of the individuation of actions and the associated picture of causation. I agree with Goldman against Davidson to the extent that I think Goldman has identified one legitimate use of 'cause', a use that is not consistent with Davidson's picture of action and causation. I am not sure that this shows that Davidson is wrong; perhaps there are merely two alternative pictures, here, pictures that do not compete with each other but are both useful, although for different purposes. Davidson's

of my saying "Hello" loudly, but this does not mean that the cause of my saying "Hello" is a cause of my saying "Hello" loudly. Similarly, we can distinguish between the cause of a desire or a belief and the cause of the desire's being felt and the belief's being occurrent. Consider one more example.

A woman bought a painting because it aroused in her a felt desire to look at it. Over the years, the initial painting lost its power to call forth a felt desire—other, newer paintings acquiring that power in the course of the woman's buying one painting after another. This is not to say that she no longer desires to look at the initial painting. Indeed, on occasion she looks at it and has a desire—even a felt desire—that that experience should occur. However, the experience never causes (or causally sustains) that felt desire. Instead, this is a typical scenario. The woman is wandering through her painting collection when she begins to think about the collection. This leads her to think of the first painting she ever bought, and in the midst of these reflections, not having paid any attention to where she is going, she suddenly finds herself looking at that first painting. She desires, *of that particular experience* that it occur, and the experience is a cause of the desire. If the woman were not having that experience, she would not desire, *of it*, that it occur. But that experience is not the cause of the desire's being felt; the cause of that is the memory-experience, not the experience of looking at the painting. If it were not for the memory-experience, the painting would have caught the woman's eye as she walked by, and she would have turned to look at it for a moment because the experience would have caused her to desire to do so. However, totally lost in thought about her painting collection, she would, after one glance, have walked on—completely unaware both of her desire to look at the painting and of the fact that she did look at it.

Examples

It is worth illustrating the definition with some examples, beginning with an example that reveals the rationale for requiring that an enjoyed experience or activity be desired *for its own sake*.

---

views are in Donald Davidson, *Essays on Actions and Events* (Oxford: The Clarendon Press, 1980); see esp. "Actions, Reasons, and Causes."

Suppose that although I am eating chocolate, I actually dislike its taste. I am eating it only because of a bet. A friend who is a gourmet cook is preparing a dessert for me that contains a trace of bittersweet chocolate, a trace I insisted that I would be able to detect. Thus the bet. When it struck me that I had never tasted bittersweet chocolate, I decided I had better eat some. So I am having the experience of tasting bittersweet chocolate. This experience causes me to believe that the concept *bittersweet* applies to it; moreover, the experience also causes me to desire of it, under the concept *bittersweet*, that it occur, for the experience makes me want the experience to continue so that I will become fully familiar with the taste. But I do not enjoy the experience, for I really do find the taste disagreeable. The requirement that what is enjoyed be desired for its own sake rules out cases such as this, for in this case I desire to eat the chocolate merely as a means to an end.

We should consider an example of enjoying an *experience* since we have focused almost exclusively on activities so far. Continuing with chocolate examples, let us suppose that you are eating a chocolate bar and enjoying the experience of tasting chocolate. When you taste the chocolate, you taste it as being a certain way. You taste it as chocolate, or as bittersweet, or as sweet, or in some other way. You don't simply taste it. Furthermore, if you taste it as bittersweet, you will believe, of your experience, that the concept *bittersweet* applies to it. This concept may also be involved in your desires. For example, I know that you do not like milk chocolate, so when I see you eating the chocolate bar, I ask in surprise what it is about this chocolate bar that makes you want it. It would be natural for you to explain that the chocolate is bittersweet and to cite the bittersweetness of the taste as what you want. You might even point out that the reason you are eating the entire bar is that the experience of the bittersweet taste makes you want to have that experience—so that as the taste fades, you eat more to preserve the experience of the bittersweet taste.

Thus it may happen that you experience tasting chocolate; that experience causes you (a) to believe, of the experience, that it realizes the concept *bittersweet*, and (b) to desire, of that experience, under the concept *bittersweet*, that it should occur for its own sake. Hence you are enjoying tasting (bittersweet) chocolate. The array of concepts involved in this example contains just the single concept

bittersweet. The above definition allows for such cases since it requires only that there be an array of concepts C and does not impose
any conditions on the size of C (except that it be nonempty). Some
experiences that we enjoy involve a large number of concepts—
watching a play, for example. In general, enjoyed experiences exhibit great variety in both the number and the types of concepts
involved.

It is worth contrasting the chocolate-bar example with a case in
which an activity, as opposed to an experience, is enjoyed but where
only a single concept is involved in the enjoyment. Suppose you
are taking a walk that you desire to take for its own sake. Then you
are walking; that activity causes you (a) to believe of it, that it
realizes the concept *walking*, and (b) to desire of it, under the
concept *walking*, that it should occur for its own sake. So you enjoy
walking. There are two points to emphasize here. First, (a) says, in
effect, that your walking causes you to believe that you are walking,
and this may sound odd. However, typically, when you are walking,
you do believe that you are, and the physical movements of walking
are certainly part of the causal ancestry of this belief; so your activity
of walking does cause you to believe that you are walking. The
second point is that it may happen that *walking* is the only concept
for which the above conditions are jointly satisified. You might be
almost completely lost in thought as you walk, so that you notice
next to nothing about where you are walking, or what you are
seeing, or how far you have gone, and so on. You are not totally
inattentive, since you must guide your steps. Moreover, you do
enjoy walking—in a muted way that provides a pleasant background to your thoughts. In such a case, *walking* might be the only
concept for which the above conditions are satisfied.

This case is analogous to the chocolate-bar case in that the relevant array of concepts C contains only the single concept of walking. But there is also an important disanalogy between the two cases.
The enjoyment in the walking case is muted, unlike the enjoyment
of the chocolate bar, which could be quite intense.[11] I suggest that
this muted enjoyment may be typical of the enjoyment of activities,
where the relevant array C contains very few concepts. Contrast the

---

11. The importance of cases involving a single concept was brought to my attention by Michael Friedman.

walking case with the deep-sea-fishing case. The array of concepts involved in your enjoyment of deep-sea fishing contains a large number of various sorts of concepts. I suggest that this sort of richness in the array of concepts is typical of full-bodied instances of the enjoyment of activities.

We could continue indefinitely with examples, for there is a wide range of diverse cases that fit the definition. However, we should turn our attention to a type of example that might be thought to cause problems for the definition. Suppose that you scratch your dog's stomach and that he enjoys the experience of being scratched—as he certainly may. It follows from the definition that there is a concept c such that the dog desires, of his experience, under c, that it occur. But it may seem obvious that this is not true, although not because dogs do not have desires. After all, we must see the dog as having desires if we describe him as enjoying something, for it seems clear that desiring is a necessary condition of enjoying; indeed, we must see the dog as having a felt desire and an occurrent belief. But this is not a problem; surely, dogs can have felt desires, and why deny that they can have something like an occurrent belief? After all, a dog can perceptually discriminate a cat from the cat's surroundings, and when it does so the perception of the cat is "before its mind" in a way that is at least roughly similar to the way that an occurrent belief is before the mind of its human believer. The problem here is not with desire, felt desire, or occurrent belief but with desire under a concept. Isn't it simply obvious, we may be asked, that dogs do not have concepts and hence that they cannot have a desire under a concept? If we answer this question yes, the dog example is a counterexample to the definition.

But the correct answer is no. A good case can be made for attributing an appropriate desire under a concept to the dog. Does this mean that dogs "have concepts"? That depends on what we mean by "having concepts." In any case, we don't need to settle this question, for to defuse the dog example it suffices to show that the dog can have an appropriate desire under a concept. We can show this in two steps, first describing a case in which a human being enjoys being scratched and then explaining why the dog example can plausibly be described in the same way.

Suppose you scratch an itch in a spot on my back that I cannot reach, and suppose I enjoy the experience of being scratched. Is there a concept *c* such that I desire, of my experience of being scratched, under *c*, that it occur? Clearly, there is, for I desire, of my experience, under the concept *being scratched*, that it occur. This desire explains why I submit to your scratching and why I protest when you stop or when your vigorous scratching turns into an unenergetic massage; in general, if I desire, of φ, under *c*, that so-and-so, this desire can be satisfied only if φ realizes *c*. Therefore, if I desire, of my experience, under the concept *being scratched*, that it occur, then this desire can be satisified only if the concept *being scratched* applies to my experience—only if my experience is one of being scratched. So it is already understandable that I should protest when I notice that your scratching has ceased or has turned into something else.

One might think that we can give an equally satisfactory explanation of my protests without employing a desire under a concept, for one might think that we need attribute to me only the desire, of my experience of being scratched, that it occur—instead of the desire, of my experience, *under the concept being scratched*, that it occur. Why isn't the former desire enough to explain my protests when your scratching stops or turns into something else? It is, after all, a desire, of my experience *of being scratched*, that it occur. So when you stop scratching or when your scratching turns into something else—like massaging—why shouldn't I protest? But this will not work. Attributing to me the desire in question could explain why I protest when you stop touching me altogether, but—as we will see—attributing this desire to me does not satisfactorily explain why I protest when your scratching becomes something else—massaging, rubbing, or whatever. I emphasize this point because it will give us a clearer picture of the dog example.

To see why the point holds, consider a case in which what I want is to feel the motion of your hands on my back. I don't care what form this motion takes—scratching, massaging, rubbing, or just a light touching. In this case, when you scratch my back, I desire, of my experiences of being scratched, that it occur. After all, the experience of being scratched is an experience of feeling the motion of your hands; and so I want it. But in this case, I will not protest if your scratching turns into a massage. I can desire, of my experience of being scratched, that it occur and yet be untroubled if the scratching turns into something else. Consequently, merely attributing to me this desire will not explain why, in our first case, I protest when your scratching becomes, for example, massaging. To explain such protests, we need to link what I desire in some essential way to being scratched. This is exactly what we accomplish by attributing to me the desire, of my experience, under the concept *being scratched*, that it occur.

Turning to the dog example, why shouldn't we describe the dog as desiring, of his experience, under the concept *being scratched*, that it occur? After all, attributing this desire to the dog explains certain aspects of his behavior. It explains why the dog submits to your scratching and why he "protests"—barks, whines, growls—when you stop, or when your scratching stops, and that his protest ceases when, and only when, your scratching resumes. Just as in the case of my being scratched, this behavior is easily explained—if we attribute to the dog the desire, of his experience, under the concept *being scratched*, that it occur. Given this attribution, the concept *being scratched* picks out a feature of the dog's experience that his experience must have if it is to satisfy his desire. Moreover, the dog is certainly capable of perceptually discriminating scratching from other things like petting, rubbing, and tickling. So when he ceases to discriminate scratching or discriminates something else such as petting, instead, he understandably "protests," that is, engages in behavior directed at having the scratching resume.

Once again, one might object that we can give an equally satisfactory explanation of the dog's "protests" without employing a desire under a concept. This is essentially the same objection we considered in the case of my being scratched, for the objection is that we can explain the dog's "protests" by attributing to him simply the desire, of his experience of being scratched, that it occur. Given this desire, why shouldn't the dog "protest" when you stop scratching or when your scratching turns into something else such as petting? This is a natural objection to raise for anyone who wishes to deny that dogs can have desires under concepts.

But the answer is the same as in the case of my being scratched. If we do attribute to the dog the desire, of his being scratched, that it occur, this attribution can explain why the dog "protests" when you stop touching him altogether, but it cannot explain why the dog "protests" when your scratching turns into something else—

petting, rubbing, or whatever. To see this, consider a case in which what the dog wants is just to feel his master's hand. A dog can certainly want such a thing: imagine a frightened dog whose whining, shivering, and incessant nuzzling of your hand cease only under your touch. Any form of touching will do. In such a case, when you scratch the dog, he certainly desires, of his experience of being scratched, that it occur. But he will not protest if your scratching turns into some other form of touching. So in our original case, we cannot explain the dog's protests merely by attributing to him the desire, of his experience of being scratched, that it occur. What we need is a closer tie between your scratching and the dog's desire, and this is precisely what we achieve by attributing to the dog the desire, of his experience, under the concept *being scratched*, that it occur. I suggest that this makes a strong case for attributing this desire to the dog. Why shouldn't we explain his behavior in this way? Indeed, what explanation is more satisfactory?

But there is one last objection, and it is that we have no real ground for assuming that it is precisely *being scratched*, and not some other concept, that is the concept under which the dog has his desire. For if c is a concept coextensive (or even just approximately coextensive) with *being scratched* we can use c to explain why the dog protests when you stop scratching and ceases to protest when, and only when, you resume. We simply attribute to the dog the desire, of his experience, under c, that it occur, and we attribute to him the perceptual ability to discriminate instances of c. Since c is coextensive with *being scratched*, this yields an explanation of the behavior in question. How do we know that c isn't the concept under which the dog has his desire? Indeed, how do we know that the concept under which the dog has his desire isn't one that we can only approximate with the words of a human language?

We can grant this objection. We set out to show only that there is some concept c such that the dog desires, of his experience, under c, that it occur; the arguments given above do make a strong case that this is so. True, these arguments focus exclusively on the concept of *being scratched*, but essentially the same arguments could be repeated for any concept coextensive (or even roughly coextensive) with *being scratched*.

A Final Objection

The definition of enjoyment uses the notion of desiring something *for its own sake*. One may object that this concept is so clear as to render the account unacceptably vague. I doubt that the concept is *unacceptably* vague, but given the use we will make of it later, one point needs clarification. This clarification should also quiet any worries about vagueness.

As a first try, let us say that to desire that p for its own sake is to desire p and not to desire it merely as a means to an end. One desires that p merely as a means to an end if and only if there is at least one end E such that one would not desire p if one did not desire E or if one did not believe that p was a means to E. For example, suppose you desire a cup of coffee. You would not desire this is you did not desire to stay awake and if you did not believe that drinking a cup of coffee was a means to staying awake. You desire the cup of coffee merely as a means to an end.

A variant of the coffee example illustrates the force of the 'merely' in "merely as a means." Again, you desire a cup of coffee. You desire to stay awake and *part* of the explanation of your desiring a cup of coffee is that you believe it is a means to staying awake. However, you would still desire a cup of coffee even if you did not desire to stay awake or if you did not believe it was a means to the desired end of staying awake, for it is 3:00 P.M.; you regularly have a cup of coffee at this time, and you have so conditioned yourself by this practice that you would desire a cup of coffee now even if you did not desire to stay awake or even if you did not believe that drinking a cup of coffee was a means to staying awake. You do not desire a cup of coffee merely as a means to an end. So in this case you count as desiring it for its own sake.

This would be an adequate account of desiring something for its own sake if it weren't for structured desires. Consider this example. Smith desires his looking at preimpressionist landscapes for its own sake, and he believes the Cézannes he is now looking at are such landscapes. This desire and belief constitute a structured desire to look at the Cézannes. Does Smith desire his looking at the Cézannes for its own sake?

According to the above definition, the answer is no. Smith would not desire to look at the Cézannes if he did not desire to look at preimpressionist landscapes or if he did not believe that looking at the Cézannes is an instance of looking at preimpressionist landscapes. So given the foregoing explanation of desiring something merely as a means, it follows that Smith desires to look at the Cézannes merely as a means to an end.

But Smith certainly desires his looking at the Cézannes for its own sake. After all, Smith desires his looking at preimpressionist landscapes for its own sake. So in desiring to look at the Cézannes, Smith is desiring precisely what he desires for its own sake. Indeed, the only way Smith can get what he desires for its own sake—that is, looking at preimpressionist landscapes—is by looking at some particular instance of such paintings, and this is why he is looking at the Cézannes. The Cézannes are, and are believed by Smith to be, preimpressionist landscapes. So looking at the Cézannes is, *qua* looking at preimpressionist landscapes, desired by Smith for its own sake. This point holds in any case in which one has a structured desire that consists of the desire for some general kind of experience or activity for its own sake and the belief that some particular experience or activity is a realization of that kind. The structured desire is a desire for that particular experience for its own sake.

So how are we to revise the explanation of what it is to desire something for its own sake so as to accommodate such cases? The key is to note that, in the coffee example, the means—drinking coffee—is *contingently related* to the end—staying awake: one can employ the means—that is, drink coffee—yet fail to achieve the end—fail to stay awake. In the Cézannes example, one cannot employ the "means"—looking at the Cézannes landscapes—and fail to achieve the end—looking at preimpressionist landscapes. Looking at the Cézannes is not a means to the end of looking at preimpressionist landscapes; to look at the Cézannes *is* to look at such landscapes. The "means" here *is* the end; more exactly, it is an instance of the end.

The way to revise the definition of desiring something for its own sake is to restrict the 'means'/'end' terminology to cases in which the means is contingently related to the end. Thus

> to desire that p for its own sake is to desire p and not to desire p merely as a (contingently related) means to an end.[12]

12. A grammatical question: what does the 'its' refer to in "for its own sake"? In

To desire that p merely as a means to an end is for there to be at least one end E such that one would not desire p if one did not desire E or did not believe that p was a—contingently related—means to E.[13]

Conclusion

Now let us turn to the question of what it is to lead a happy life. My claim is that the central component of a happy life is a *special kind* of enjoyment, an enjoyment intimately connected with exercising one's ability to act freely. The next chapter begins by offering an account of this special kind of enjoyment.

---

writing "one desires that p for its own sake," I am assuming that the 'its' refers to the proposition p. It is a certain state of affairs—p's obtaining—that one desires for its own sake. Every use I make of the notion of desire for its own sake could be cast in this propositional form. But I will not do so and will even allow myself 'desires to φ for its own sake' where, on the face of it, the 'its' refers back (ungrammatically) to an infinitive.

13. It is worth appending two examples of desiring something merely as a means to an end. The first is a case in which something is E-desired merely as a means to an end. Suppose I E-desire social prestige. I happen to believe that being an active member of a yacht club is a means to social prestige, and I also believe that realizing the self-concept *being a sailor* is a means to being an active member of a yacht club. These two beliefs and the E-desire constitute a structured desire to realize the self-concept *being a sailor*. I desire this merely as a means to an end since I would not have the structured desire to realize the self-concept if I did not have the E-desire and the beliefs about means that are the components of that desire. Without the structured desire, I would not have any desire to realize the self-concept. By way of contrast, consider a second example in which something is desired merely as a means to an end, and the desire is not a structured desire. Suppose Smith desires to quench his thirst; he believes that drinking water is the best means of doing this. This desire is a third psychological state; separate and distinct from the desire and the belief. It is not a structured desire consisting of Smith's desire to quench his thirst and the belief that water is a means. Smith nonetheless desires to drink water merely as a means to an end for if he ceased to desire to quench his thirst, or ceased to believe that water was a means for doing so, his desire to drink water would disappear.

5 Enjoyment and Happiness

The idea that enjoyment is a central component of happiness is hardly new. As we noted in the Introduction, Sidgwick says that by 'the greatest possible Happiness', he understands "the greatest attainable surplus of pleasure over pain; the two terms being used, with equally comprehensive meanings, to include respectively all kinds of agreeable and disagreeable feelings."[1] Unlike Sidgwick, I think that a *special kind* of enjoyment is the central component of happiness. My view is more like Aristotle's, who also holds that a special kind of enjoyment—the enjoyment associated with virtuous action—is involved in a happy life. He contends that

> actions which conform to virtue are naturally pleasant, and, as a result, such actions are not only pleasant for those who love the noble but also pleasant in themselves. The life of such men has no further need of pleasure as an added attraction but contains pleasure in itself.[2]

1. Henry Sidgwick, *The Methods of Ethics*, 7th ed. (Indianapolis/Cambridge, Mass.: Hackett, 1981), pp. 120–121.
2. *Nicomachean Ethics*, 1099a13–22. The translation (here and throughout) is Martin Ostwald's: *Nicomachean Ethics* (Indianapolis: Bobbs-Merrill, 1962).

Such "pleasures . . . complete the activities of a perfect or complete and supremely happy man."[3] I differ from Aristotle in taking the special kind of enjoyment to be associated not with virtue but with the exercise of the ability to act freely.

Three Preliminary Points

To draw the connections between freedom and enjoyment, we first need to note three points.

1. The first point follows immediately from the definition of the ability to act freely given in Chapter 2: a necessary condition of exercising the ability to act freely is acting self-consciously on an E-desire to continue to realize a self-concept for its own sake.

2. The second point follows from the definition of desiring something for its own sake. As a preliminary, recall that to act on an E-desire to continue to realize a self-concept is to be caused to act by a structured desire consisting of the E-desire and a belief. The belief may be a belief to the effect either that some experience or activity *realizes* a self-concept or that some experience or activity is a *means* to realizing a self-concept. Suppose that in the first case, the "realization" case, the component E-desire is a desire to realize the self-concept for its own sake. Then—and this is the second point—the structured desire is also a desire for experience or activity for its own sake. This is not true in the second case, the "means" case. Our focus is on the realization cases—on structured desires, where the component belief is a belief about realization. As we will see later, these cases stand in a special relation to enjoyment (precisely because the structured desire is a desire for something for its own sake).

3. We need to be more precise than we have been so far in describing the content of such structured desires. The "of φ under c" terminology introduced in the last chapter yields the necessary precision. Suppose that Jones has a structured desire consisting of the E-desire to continue to realize the expansive self-concept *riding spirited horses* for its own sake and the belief that riding Dancer realizes this self-concept. This structured desire is satisfied only if

3. Ibid., 1176a26–27.

his riding Dancer realizes the concept *riding spirited horses*. If he were to find that Dancer was actually a docile horse, he would regard himself as not having received what he wanted, for the structured desire consists, in part, of the E-desire to continue to realize the self-concept *riding spirited horses*, and what the E-desire/belief pair motivates him to do is to ride Dancer as a way of realizing that self-concept. We can express this involvement of the self-concept in Jones's desire by saying that he desires, of riding Dancer, under the self-concept *riding spirited horses*, that it occur. To summarize: to exercise the ability to act freely is (in part) to act self-consciously on an E-desire to realize an expansive self-concept for its own sake. To act on such a desire is to be caused to act by a structured desire consisting of the E-desire and an appropriate belief. In the case in which the belief is a belief to the effect that some experience or activity realizes the self-concept, we can describe the structured desire as a desire, of φ, under the self-concept, that it occur for its own sake.

A Special Kind of Enjoyment

Suppose that one exercises one's ability to act freely and thus acts self-consciously on an E-desire to realize a self-concept for its own sake, where the component belief of the relevant structured desire is a belief to the effect that some experience or activity realizes the self-concept. In such a case, to act self-consciously on an E-desire is almost to satisfy the conditions necessary and sufficient for enjoyment. To see why is to see the essential connection between freedom and enjoyment.

Consider an example. I am waxing my boat; in doing so, I am acting self-consciously on my E-desire to continue to realize the self-concept *being a sailor* for its own sake. For me to act on an E-desire is for me to be caused to act by a structured desire consisting of the E-desire and an appropriate belief. In this case, the relevant structured desire consists of my belief that waxing the boat realizes the self-concept *being a sailor* and the E-desire to continue to realize that self-concept. This belief/desire pair constitutes the structured desire, of waxing the boat, under the self-concept *being a sailor*, that it occur for its own sake. I act *self-consciously* on the E-desire if and only if the structured desire (which causes me to act) is a felt desire; the component E-desire is a felt desire, and the component belief, an occurrent belief.

To summarize:

(1) I am waxing the boat;
(2) (a) I believe occurrently that waxing the boat realizes the self-concept *being a sailor*; (b) I have the felt structured desire, of waxing the boat, under that self-concept, that it occur, where this structured desire consists of the belief specified in (a) and the felt E-desire to realize the self-concept *being a sailor* for its own sake.

Note that the structured desire to wax the boat is a desire to wax the boat for its own sake since: (i) the component E-desire is a desire to realize the self-concept for its own sake, and (ii) the component belief is a belief to the effect that waxing the boat realizes the self-concept.

With just one addition, these conditions entail (but are not entailed by) the conditions that define enjoyment. The addition is that the requisite causal relations obtain. Indicating the addition by boldface type, we have:

first, I am waxing the boat; second, **my waxing the boat causes me**:
(a) to believe occurrently that waxing the boat realizes the self-concept *being a sailor*;
(b) to have the felt structured desire, of waxing the boat, under the self-concept, that it occur, where the structured desire consists of the belief specified in (a) and the felt E-desire to realize the self-concept for its own sake.

These conditions clearly entail, but are not entailed by, the definition of enjoyment. So in a realization case, to act self-consciously on an E-desire is *almost* to satisfy the definition of enjoyment: one will satisfy that definition if the requisite causal relations hold. This means also that to exercise the ability to act freely is—in the realization cases—almost to satisfy the definition of enjoyment. To exercise the ability to act freely is to act self-consciously on a desire,

so to exercise the ability is—in the appropriate realization case—
almost to satisfy the definition of enjoyment.[4]

My claim is that the above conditions describe a special kind of
enjoyment—call it 'the enjoyment of realizing a self-concept'.

> A person enjoys the realization of a self-concept c at a time t
> if and only if:
>
>> (1) the person engages in an activity or has an experience
>> φ at t' (a time slightly prior to t), and
>> (2) his φing causes him at t:
>> (a) to believe occurrently that φ realizes c;
>> (b) to have the felt structured desire, of φ, under c, that it occur,
>> where the structured desire consists of the belief that φ realizes
>> c and the felt E-desire to realize c for its own sake.

Why single out this sort of enjoyment as a special kind? The main
reason is the role that this sort of enjoyment plays in leading
a happy life, but there is another reason—relatively independent
of considerations about happiness—that is worth noting first:
such enjoyments instantiate an essential feature of enjoyment
twice.

Consider that every enjoyment involves a certain sort of occurrent
belief and a certain sort of felt desire. In the boat example, the
relevant occurrent belief is the belief that my waxing the boat realizes the self-concept *being a sailor*; the relevant felt desire is the
structured desire, of the activity of waxing the boat, under the self-
concept, that it occur. Given this belief, I experience the satisfaction
of the desire: I have the occurrent belief at the same time that I
have the felt desire.

The enjoyment of realizing a self-concept exhibits an additional
experience of the satisfaction of desire. In the waxing the boat
example, I also E-desire to realize the self-concept *being a sailor*.
This is a felt desire, so given my occurrent belief that waxing the

---

4. So there would seem to be some truth in Aristotle's observation that "Pleasure
completes the activity not as a characteristic completes an activity by being already
inherent in it, but as a completeness that superimposes itself upon it, like the bloom
of youth in those who are in their prime" (1174b32–35). To act self-consciously on
an E-desire is almost to enjoy the realization of a self-concept; if the causal requirement is met, one could describe this as a completion of the activity, "a completeness
that superimposes itself upon it."

boat realizes the self-concept, I will experience the satisfaction of that desire. Again, I have the occurrent belief and at the same time have the felt desire.

It is not completely accurate to say that I experience the satisfaction of the E-desire. What I experience is the partial satisfaction of that desire. The E-desire is a desire to realize the expansive self-concept, *being a sailor*. An expansive self-concept is realizable over time by a temporally extended series of experiences and activities, and the E-desire is a desire for such a series. No single experience or activity can completely satisfy such a desire. When I occurrently believe that waxing the boat realizes the self-concept *being a sailor* while at the same time having the felt desire to continue to realize that self-concept, it seems to me as if I am getting part of what I want. There is a sharp contrast here with my desire, of the activity of waxing the boat, under the self-concept, that it occur. I experience the complete satisfaction of that desire since what I want is the particular activity that I believe to be occurring.

In general, whenever an expansive self-concept is involved in the enjoyment of the realization of a self-concept, one experiences the complete satisfaction of one desire and the partial satisfaction of another. This double experience of complete and partial satisfaction gives such enjoyments a distinctive experiential quality. This distinctive quality is one reason for singling out such enjoyments as a special kind, for the enjoyment characterized by this quality figures importantly in our lives. The examples that follow illustrate this point.

You are being held as a political prisoner. Prison conditions are squalid and unsanitary, and far from having any hope of release, you think it most likely that you will be executed. Still, you are sustained by the thought that the government has made a serious mistake; your political martyrdom will be the beginning of their downfall. The government compounds its mistake by allowing you to make a long and impassioned speech at your mock trial. You enjoy making the speech, and this enjoyment is the enjoyment of realizing the self-concept *political activist*. A certain melancholy accompanies this enjoyment, for the enjoyment involves an E-desire to continue to realize an expansive self-concept, and you know that the continuation is impossible. Nonetheless, you have the double experience of satisfaction when you make the speech, for in making it you are acting self-consciously on your E-desire to continue to realize the self-concept *political activist*.

A final example. Imagine Jones when he was young reading the following lines from Dylan Thomas:

> The force that through the green fuse drives the flower
> Drives my green age; that blasts the roots of trees
> Is my destroyer.
> I am dumb to tell the crooked rose
> My youth is bent by the same wintry fever.[5]

Jones enjoyed reading the lines, and the enjoyment was the enjoyment of realizing a self-concept, for he E-desired to realize the self-concept *seeing himself in such-and-such a way.* Compare his reading the lines now—fifteen years later, having happened across them accidentally while leafing through a collection of poetry. The lines still express his youthful concerns, and he still enjoys reading them. But he does not enjoy them in the same way: his youthful enjoyment was the enjoyment of realizing a self-concept; his present enjoyment, merely the product of a sudden illumination of memory as reading the lines makes the almost forgotten concerns of his youth once more fully vivid before his mind. Recognizing in the lines a way he used to see himself, he is struck by how much he has changed.

In regard to the role of this special kind of enjoyment in happiness, my claim is that one is leading a happy life only if one enjoys the realization of self-concepts to which one is committed. Seeing this is the key to giving an account of leading a happy life.

Enjoyment and Happiness

Consider Jane, a businesswoman committed to realizing a certain collection C of expansive self-concepts. One of these concepts— *exercising power*—plays a central and unifying role in C, the other members of C being concepts such as *being president of the company, managing personnel well,* and *drawing a large salary.* Jane has successfully realized these concepts for a number of years, and

5. Dylan Thomas, "The Force That through the Green Fuse Drives the Flower," *Collected Poems* (New York: New Directions, 1957), p. 10.

as a result she has, until now, led a happy life. She is still living her life just as before, committed to realizing the same collection of self-concepts and realizing them just as successfully. Her desires, beliefs, hopes, fears, patterns of emotional reaction, personal loyalties, character traits, and so on are essentially the same; at least there has been no dramatic, noticeable change. Yet she is no longer leading a happy life, for her life is deficient in enjoyment; indeed, she spends virtually all of her time doing things she does not enjoy. The reason is that although she used to enjoy the experiences and activities that realize her self-concepts, she now no longer does.

A life can grow stale in this way; cases of this sort are not uncommon. But they are puzzling. Why, seemingly without any essential change in one's beliefs, desires, hopes, fears, and so on, should one cease to enjoy the experiences and activities that one previously enjoyed, experiences and activities that realize concepts to which one remains committed? The definition of enjoying the realization of a self-concept provides the basis for an answer. Compare two instances of the same activity—one occurring before Jane is unhappy; the other, after.

The first instance. Jane promotes Charles. In doing so, she is acting self-consciously on her E-desire to continue to realize the expansive self-concept *exercising power*. Acting on this E-desire, Jane enjoys the realization of the self-concept. That is, the following conditions hold: (1) Jane promotes Charles; (2) this causes Jane (a) to believe occurrently that the activity of promoting Charles realizes the self-concept *exercising power*, and (b) to have the felt structured desire, of that activity, under the self-concept, that it occur, where the structured desire consists of the belief specified in (a) and the felt E-desire to continue to realize the self-concept for its own sake. In satisfying these conditions, Jane has the double experience of satisfaction that is characteristic of the enjoyment of realizing a self-concept.

The second instance. Jane promotes Charles again, and in doing so she is again acting self-consciously on her E-desire to realize the self-concept *exercising power*, but this time she does not enjoy the realization of that self-concept. This means that Jane's promoting Charles fails to fulfill the causal condition in the definition of enjoying the realization of a self-concept, for given that she acts self-consciously on her E-desire, she fulfills all the other conditions. So the activity of promoting Charles must fail to cause (or causally sustain) either the felt structured desire or the occurrent belief.

Failure to cause the felt desire.   Suppose that when Jane promotes Charles, she desires, of that activity, under the self-concept *exercising power*, that it occur. In addition, the activity is a cause of the desire, for if Jane were not engaging in that particular activity, she would not desire, *of it*, that it occur. However, the activity is not the cause of the desire's *being felt*. That cause consists in certain of Jane's thoughts and reflections—thoughts and reflections that begin just before her calling Charles in to tell him of his promotion. Jane plays out in her imagination a picture of herself as exercising power, a picture that fascinates her; the picture lingers in her mind when Charles walks in, and the picture is the source of the desire's being felt.

Had the picture not lingered, Jane would have simply noted that the time for her meeting with Charles had come, and she would merely have thought, "It's time to promote Charles." This thought would have occupied her attention; although she would still have been moved to act by her desire, of promoting Charles, under the self-concept *exercising power*, that it occur, the desire would not have been felt. This would have happened because Jane finds activities like promoting Charles too familiar, routine, and unchallenging. The imagined picture of herself as exercising power still fascinates her, but the actual experiences and activities in which she does so have lost the power to cause *felt* desires. This is why Jane fails to enjoy promoting Charles, for to enjoy is to respond in a certain way, and an essential feature of this response is the causing of a felt desire.

Suppose that all (or almost all) of the experiences and activities that realize self-concepts to which Jane is committed fail to cause the relevant felt desires. The result is that although Jane devotes virtually all of her time to realizing the self-concepts to which she is committed, this expenditure of time and effort yields no enjoyment. Jane is not leading a happy life, for a happy life is not deficient in enjoyment, and Jane's life is so deficient. So it would seem that the enjoyment of realizing a self-concept is a necessary condition of leading a happy life.

But there is an obvious and important objection. Why couldn't Jane compensate for the loss of the enjoyment of realizing the self-concepts to which she is committed by seeking out other enjoyments, enjoyments that do not involve realizing self-concepts to which she is committed? Janes does not, after all, have to devote all of her time to realizing the self-concepts to which she is committed. Imagine that Jane, who always tended toward being a gourmand, throws herself into the enjoyment of food and drink. This enjoyment might be simply *plain* enjoyment, an enjoyment that merely meets the conditions given in the previous chapter; or it might be that Jane E-desires to realize the self-concept *being a gourmand* and that her enjoyment is the enjoyment of realizing a self-concept. But the point is that—in either case—she is not enjoying the realization of a self-concept to which she is committed. She was never, and is not now, committed to realizing the self-concept *being a gourmand*. But despite the absence of commitment, let us suppose that Jane enjoys food and drink throughout the day, every day, so that her life is filled with enjoyment. Why isn't this enough to compensate for the loss of the enjoyment of realizing self-concepts to which she is committed?

Because of the nature of commitment. Here are the relevant facts. Jane is committed to realizing the self-concepts in the collection C. But suppose that Jane believes that to realize those self-concepts sufficiently often, she must forgo her usual leisurely lunch at the French restaurant to chair a noon business meeting. Given her commitment, Jane will (barring eventualities such as lack of need, unexpected opportunity, inattention, carelessness, being overpowered by a desire, and so on) exercise her ability to act freely so as to ensure that she acts in accord with this belief, thereby ensuring that she abandons the enjoyment of the leisurely lunch for the sake of realizing her self-concepts. This follows from the definition of commitment. To be committed to realizing the self-concepts in C sufficiently often is: (1) regularly to form beliefs as to how to realize one's self-concepts sufficiently often and (2) to exercise one's ability to act freely to (try to) ensure that one acts on one's E-desires in the order specified in such beliefs (barring eventualities such as lack of need, unexpected opportunity, inattention, carelessness, and being overpowered by a desire). It follows from (2) that Jane will—barring the aforementioned eventualities—forgo the leisurely lunch and the enjoyment it involves to chair the noon business meeting.

We can express the fact that Jane will abandon the activities she enjoys to engage in those self-concept-realizing activities that she does not enjoy by saying that she values the latter more than the former. In this sense, to value A over B is to have a standing commitment to selecting A over B in cases of conflict; this is certainly one sense, although undoubtedly not the only one—of 'to value'.[6] By 'commitment' here I mean commitment in the sense just explained above—the sense of commitment defined in Chapter 3. Thus, valuing in this sense is something built into one by virtue of one's being a person since commitment to self-concepts is a necessary condition of personhood. Note that in defining valuing in terms of commitment, we have (as I promised in Chapter 2) defined valuing in terms of the ability to act freely: freedom is the ultimate source of valuing.

To return to Jane, she is trying to replace the enjoyment of activities she values more with the enjoyment of activities she values less. This is why Jane's enjoyment of food and drink is not enough to compensate for the loss of the enjoyment of realizing self-concepts to which she is committed; for in the happy life, one enjoys what one values more, rather than what one values less. There is a connection here with Aristotle's remark (quoted at the beginning) that "the life of [virtuous] men has no further need of pleasure as an added attraction but contains pleasure in itself"; in a happy life, meeting the commitment to realizing self-concepts "contains pleasure in itself" since one enjoys what one values. One does not need to seek enjoyment from other sources as an "added attraction."[7]

6. Compare Watson: "We might say that an agent's values consist in those principles and ends which he—in a cool and non-self-deceptive moment—articulates as definitive of the good, fulfilling, and defensible life." Gary Watson, "Free Agency," in Gary Watson, ed., *Free Will* (New York: Oxford University Press, 1982). One can value something in the sense defined in the text without it being a part of what one would articulate "as definitive of the good, fulfilling, and defensible life." One's actual commitments need not match one's sincere, nonself-deceptive opinion about the good.

7. Compare two points Aristotle makes. First, he holds that "pleasure is a necessary ingredient in happiness" (*Nicomachean Ethics*, 1177a23) but also that not

Indeed, one is—almost—assured of enjoying what one values since one will exercise the ability to act freely in order to meet one's commitment to realizing self-concepts sufficiently often, and so to exercise the ability to act freely in this way is—almost—to enjoy the realization of self-concepts to which one is committed. Only the causal condition remains to be fulfilled; one only needs, as it were, the causal cooperation of the world.

This completes my discussion of the case in which there is a failure to cause the felt desire. In regard to the failure to cause the occurrent belief, the considerations do not differ in any essential way from the desire case, so I will be brief.

Failure to cause the occurrent belief. As in the desire example, Jane, before calling Charles in, is playing out in her imagination a picture of her as someone who possesses and exercises power over others—the picture that fascinates her. When Charles comes into his office, Jane believes, of the activity of promoting Charles, that it realizes the self-concept *exercising power*; in addition, activity is a cause of this belief. The belief is also an occurrent belief, but the activity is not a cause of the belief's being occurrent. The cause of that is the imagined picture that lingers on in Jane's mind when Charles comes in. If Jane did not still have this picture in her mind, she would have called Charles in, and she would have believed that in promoting Charles she was exercising power, but this belief

---

just any kind of pleasure is relevant, for example: "happiness does not consist in amusement. In fact it would be strange if our end were amusement, and if we were to labor and suffer hardships all our life long merely to amuse ourselves. For, one might say, we choose everything for the sake of something else—happiness; for happiness is an end. Obviously, it is foolish and all too childish to exert serious efforts and toil for the purposes of amusement" (1176b28–33). Second, when discussing the relation between happiness and intelligence (*nous*), Aristotle says: "One might even regard it [intelligence] as each man's true self, since it is the controlling and better part. . . . Moreover, what we stated before will apply here too: what is by nature proper to each thing will be at once the best and the most pleasant for it. In other words, a life guided by intelligence is the best and most pleasant for man, inasmuch as intelligence, above all else, is man. Consequently this kind of life is happiest" (1178a1–7). On my account not just any enjoyment is relevant to whether one is leading a happy life; it has to be the enjoyment of realizing a self-concept to which one is committed. Although commitment to self-concept is part of what makes one the person one is, this notion of personhood differs markedly from Aristotle's notion of the true self, for if "each man's true self" is intelligence, each man's true self is the same as every other man's.

would not have been occurrent. As in the desire example, the imagined picture still fascinates Jane, but the actual experiences and activities in which she exercises power have become so routine, familiar, and unchallenging that they have no hold on her attention, having lost the power to cause the relevant occurrent beliefs. So just as in the desire case, Jane's life is deficient in enjoyment, and so she does not count as leading a happy life.

In light of these considerations, I suggest that

> One is leading a happy life only if one enjoys the realization
> of the self-concepts to which one is committed.

This makes acting self-consciously on E-desires a necessary condition of leading a happy life since so acting is a necessary condition of enjoying the realization of a self-concept. It is worth giving an example that illustrates the intuitive appeal of this result. Imagine when it is time to promote Charles that Jane is extremely busy. She does not call Charles in to tell him of his promotion; instead, she simply hurriedly signs the relevant papers when her secretary puts them on her desk. When she signs the papers, she does not occurrently believe that promoting Charles realizes the self-concept *exercising power*, nor is her E-desire to realize that self-concept a felt desire. Suppose this happens throughout Jane's life; that is, she is so overworked and distracted that she rarely acts self-consciously on her E-desires to realize the self-concepts to which she is committed. The result is that her life is almost totally lacking in the enjoyment of realizing self-concepts, so if this sort of enjoyment is a necessary condition of happiness, she is not leading a happy life. Intuitively, this seems right; the life of overwork to the point of distraction is not a happy one.

Let us assume that the enjoyment of realizing a self-concept is a necessary condition of leading a happy life. But how much enjoyment of this sort is required? One can fail to lead a happy life because enjoyments of the right sort as too few and far between. So how much enjoyment does the happy life require?

Leading a Happy Life

One is leading a happy life only if one enjoys *sufficiently often* the realization of those self-concepts to which one is committed.

To be more precise, first recall that one is a person only if the total period of time T during which one exists divides into periods T_1, ...,T_n such that each T_i is a maximal period of commitment. Diagramatically:

I will first give conditions for leading a happy life during a maximal period of commitment. Later I will consider how to build out to a general account of what it is to lead a happy life. This provides a solution to the problem raised in the Introduction of how to demarcate the periods of time for which it makes sense to raise the question of whether one is leading a happy life. Let T be a maximal period commitment and C be the collection of self-concepts one is committed to throughout T. Then, I suggest:

> one is leading a happy life during T only if, during T, one enjoys the realization of the self-concepts in C sufficiently often.

In assessing the plausibility of this condition, bear in mind the explanation of 'sufficiently often' given in Chapter 3: to realize the self-concepts in C sufficiently often is to realize them with a certain frequency, where this frequency should be thought of as an approximately specifiable range of (precisely specificable) frequencies, where even the upper and lower bounds of the range may also be vague and only approximately specifiable. Suppose that the self-concept realizing experiences and activities that one enjoys fall clearly outside the lower bound of this frequency range. The claim is that then one's life is deficient in enjoyment. So understood, I take the necessity of the condition to be extremely plausible; surely, it is one's own commitment to realizing self-concepts that determines what counts, in one's own case, as enough enjoyment—that is, enough for happiness.

It is tempting to take the above condition as sufficient. To do so would be to endorse a variant of Sidgwick's view that happiness consists in a sufficient surplus of pleasure over pain. We would not be following Sidgwick in using the terms 'pleasure' and 'pain' with "equally comprehensive meanings, to include respectively all kinds of agreeable and disagreeable feelings"; but otherwise the view would merely be a refinement of Sidgwick's proposal. However, attractive as it is in its simplicity, the above "Sidgwickian condition"—as I shall refer to it—is not sufficient.

To see why, suppose Mason is a gourmet who makes his living as a restaurant reviewer for newspapers and magazines. He is committed to realizing a certain collection *C* of self-concepts; *C* includes *being a gourmet, appreciating fine French food, appreciating fine wine*, and so on. Mason is realizing these concepts sufficiently often, and he enjoys their realization. But he is not leading a happy life. He is despondent and gloomy and at times even distraught, for he has gout, and his doctor has convinced him that he must begin, and permanently adhere to, a rigid diet that proscribes all gourmet food. He has decided to begin the diet soon, and so he expects that he will cease to realize the self-concepts to which he is committed. This expectation is the source of his despair. His last indulgences in gourmet food occur against a background of gloom—precisely because he is acutely aware that they are his last indulgences. During these last indulgences, he enjoys the realization of the self-concepts to which he is committed, but, even in the midst of this enjoyment, he is not free of his despair.[8] Mason satisfies the Sidgwickian condition, but he is certainly not leading a happy life.

What the condition fails to capture is the motivational dimension of the concept of happiness. As we argued in the Introduction, the happy person has an "affirmative attitude" toward his life, where this attitude serves as a motive to realize the self-concepts to which the person is committed. What we need to add to the Sidgwickian

8. One might object that Mason, miserable as he is, cannot enjoy his gourmet indulgences. But this is wrong; it is possible for Mason to satisfy the conditions given earlier for enjoying the realization of a self-concept. What makes it seem that Mason cannot enjoy the indulgences is a certain equivocation on 'enjoy'. Sometimes when one says, "I enjoy it," one may suggest or imply that the enjoyment is 'pure'—unmixed with any significant degree of pain, distaste, or aversion. For example, I enjoy gossiping about my colleagues, but I also hate myself for doing so. When I yield to the temptation to gossip, my enjoyment coexists with a gnawing sense of shame. If you ask me, "Are you enjoying gossiping?" it would be misleading of me to answer simply yes. That would suggest that my enjoyment was untainted by any admixture of aversion. This does not mean it is false that I enjoy gossiping; it just means my answer must take the form "Yes, but . . . " Similarly, Mason can enjoy his last indulgences even though this enjoyment coexists with his gloom.

condition is the requirement that one have this "affirmative attitude." To do this, we need to say exactly what the attitude is. The
Mason example suggests that the affirmative attitude is an expectation—in particular, the expectation that one will realize sufficiently often the self-concepts to which one is committed. Mason,
after all, is unhappy because he has the opposite expectation. So
why not hold that happiness requires that one expect to realize
one's self-concepts?

With one qualification, which I will suppress for now, I think
this is correct—indeed, correct on an especially rich reading of what
'expects' means in this context. The concept of commitment is the
key to seeing that the suggestion is correct. Here the important point
about commitment is that a necessary condition of commitment to
realizing a collection of self-concepts sufficiently often is that one
should regularly form beliefs as to how to realize the self-concepts
sufficiently often. The precise meaning of the phrase "beliefs as to
how to realize one's self-concepts sufficiently often" is relevant. In
Chapter 3 we introduced the phrase to cover both the case in which
one believes that one will (or is likely to) realize one's self-concepts
sufficiently often and the case in which one thinks that the best
one can do is some (possibly very remote) approximation. To return
to Mason, since he is committed to realizing a certain collection of
self-concepts, he will form beliefs as to how to realize those self-
concepts sufficiently often.

What will be the character of these beliefs if Mason is to count
as leading a happy life? I contend that he must regularly form beliefs
as to how to realize his self-concepts *sufficiently often*. It will be
convenient to have a concise way to express the fact that Mason
forms such beliefs. One natural way to do this is to give a special
sense to 'expects to realize sufficiently often the self-concepts to
which he is committed'. Let us from now on understand this to
mean that one regularly forms beliefs as to how to realize one's self-
concepts sufficiently often. So to say that Mason expects to realize
his self-concepts sufficiently often is to attribute to him not just
one single expectation but a whole array of beliefs. Nonetheless, it
is expositionally convenient, and philosophically harmless, to talk
as if we were dealing with a single expectation.

It is important to be clear about the precise content of this expectation. To this end, recall (one more time) that to realize self-

concepts sufficiently often is to realize them with a certain frequency—this frequency being an approximately specifiable range
of (precisely specificable) frequencies. So when Mason expects to
realize the self-concepts sufficiently often, he expects his self-concept-realizing activities to fall clearly within the bounds of the
relevant frequency range. Contrast expecting merely to approximate
to realizing his self-concepts sufficiently often. This would be to
expect the self-concept-realizing experiences and activities to fall
clearly outside the lower bound of the relevant frequency range.
To have this expectation is to foresee failure—failure to meet a
standard defined and imposed on one by one's own commitment,
the standard of realizing self-concepts sufficiently often. Surely, the
happy person does not expect such failure. When the happy person
projects his future by forming beliefs as to how to realize his self-
concepts sufficiently often, he does not project failure but success:
he expects to realize the self-concepts sufficiently often. This expectation is—subject to the qualification I am suppressing—the affirmative attitude. Or so I claim.

One might object that I am ignoring a point emphasized in the
Introduction. There we argued that we could not account for the
explanatory role of "Because it makes him/her happy" unless we
recognized that the affirmative attitude serves as a motive to live
one's life in a certain way. Does the expectation in question serve
as a motive to realize self-concepts sufficiently often? If so, its claim
to being the affirmative attitude would be greatly substantiated. If
not, it would seem that we should reject its claim to that role.

In fact, the expectation always serves as a motive to realize self-
concepts sufficiently often; indeed, this follows from the definition
of commitment. Our talk here of an expectation is really talk of a
collection of beliefs, where each belief is a belief about some specific
order in which to realize one's self-concepts. What I will show is
that each of the relevant beliefs must serve as a motive to realize
the self-concepts in that order. But isn't there a difficulty here? We
have not given a definition of what is to be a motive, so how am I
going to show that the beliefs always qualify as motives? I take it
to be sufficient to show that such beliefs always possess two central
and fundamental features of motives: they are typically causes of
action, and they are—other things being equal—justifications of
action.

Suppose I believe that by acting in such-and-such a way I will realize sufficiently often the self-concepts to which I am committed. It follows from the definition of commitment that the belief is typically a cause of action. Here the important feature of commitment is that I am committed to realizing the self-concepts sufficiently often only if I exercise my ability to act freely to (try to) ensure that I realize the self-concepts in the order specified in my beliefs as to how to realize the self-concepts sufficiently often (barring eventualities such as lack of need, unexpected opportunity, inattention, carelessness, being overpowered by a desire, and so on). Thus given that I believe that by acting in such-and-such a way I will realize my self-concepts sufficiently often, I am such that—barring certain eventualities—I will exercise my ability to act freely so as to ensure that I act in accord with this belief. So given my commitment, the belief typically will cause action.

The belief is also, other things being equal, a justification for action. The reason is that personhood requires that one's mental life exhibit a certain order, an order imposed through one's exercise of one's ability to act freely so as to realize self-concepts to which one is committed. The belief that one can realize the self-concepts by acting in such-and-such a way is surely—other things being equal—a justification for so acting: one's existence as a person is at stake. Other things being equal, one is justified in doing what preserves one's existence.

So, the expectation that one will realize sufficiently often the self-concepts to which one is committed is a motive to realize those self-concepts sufficiently often, and this is a good reason to think that the expectation is the affirmative attitude. But—and this is the qualification that I have been suppressing—we should not identify the affirmative attitude with merely having the motivating expectation.

To see why, consider that, like any motive, the expectation provides a justification only if other things are equal, and as is the case with any motive, one may or may not take it to provide a justification for action; it depends on whether one regards other things as equal. Now, if one is leading a happy life, what will one's attitude be as to whether the motivating expectation provides a justification? A necessary condition of leading a happy life is that one not only expects to realize one's self-concepts sufficiently often but that one also take this motivating expectation to be a justification for doing so. For this reason, we should require that the motivating expectation qualifies as the affirmative attitude only if one takes the motive provided by that expectation to be a justification for realizing one's self-concepts sufficiently often.

To argue for these claims, let us return to Mason. In his pre-gout life, Mason is committed to realizing a certain collection of self-concepts (the collection that includes *being a gourmet*, *appreciating fine French food*, and *appreciating fine wine*), and he expects to continue to realize these self-concepts sufficiently often. Given Mason's commitment, this expectation must, as we have just seen, serve as a motive. But suppose that Mason does not take this motive to provide a justification for realizing his self-concepts. Other beliefs serves as motives, and Mason takes *these* beliefs to provide justifications for action. These other beliefs are beliefs *as to how* to realize his self-concepts sufficiently often, but none of them is a belief that he *will* realize those self-concepts sufficiently often; rather, they are beliefs as to how merely to approximate to that standard. There are a variety of reasons why this might happen.

Mental disorder is one possibility. Mason might suffer from a personality disorder that makes him think he deserves punishment; because of this he thinks that he does not deserve to realize his self-concepts sufficiently often but should punish himself by not realizing them sufficiently often. Another possibility is that Mason thinks he has duties to others—his children, perhaps—that require a course of action that entails forgoing the realization of his self-concepts sufficiently often. The exact explanation of Mason's situation does not really matter. What is important is that, given his commitment, Mason will act on the "approximation" beliefs, not on the "sufficiently often" belief. To see why, consider that his commitment is a commitment to use his ability to act freely to ensure that he acts on beliefs as to how to realize his self-concepts. The ability to act freely is (in part) the ability to act on motivating conceptions that one takes to be justifications for action. In the case at hand, the motivating conceptions Mason takes to be justifications for action are the "approximation" beliefs, not the "sufficiently often" belief; so, because of his commitment, he will act on the former beliefs instead of the latter. Thus Mason is committed to realizing a collection of self-concepts sufficiently often; yet he is enjoined—by virtue of that very commitment—to forgo realizing the self-concepts sufficiently often. Such a self-defeating life is not a happy one.

I conclude then that one is leading a happy life only if one not only expects to realize one's self-concepts sufficiently often but also takes this motivating expectation to be a justification for doing so. Can we, then, identify the affirmative attitude with the motivating expectation that one will realize one's self-concepts sufficiently often, where this expectation is taken to be a justification for doing so? Not quite. Consider a variation of the Mason example. Mason is not afflicted with the gout but with a neurological condition that will soon destroy his ability to discriminate among tastes. When he learns of his condition, Mason's reaction is to reaffirm his commitment to his gourmet way of life. The result is that he not only expects to continue to realize his self-concepts sufficiently often; he also takes this motivating expectation to be a justification for continuing to realize those self-concepts. He does this because he thinks of himself as a badly injured warrior who, although doomed to defeat, nonetheless defiantly refuses to cease struggling in pursuit of an unobtainable ideal—the ideal for the gourmet Mason being the refinement of appetite as a source of pleasure. However, Mason, because of his neurological condition, does not expect to continue to enjoy realizing his self-concepts. This is enough to throw him into despair so that his last—enjoyed—indulgences in gourmet food occur against a background of gloom. Filled with despair, he is not leading a happy life.

We could avoid this counterexample simply by identifying the affirmative attitude with the motivating expectation that one will realize, and enjoy realizing, the self-concepts to which one is committed, where one takes this expectation to be a justification for doing so. But do so only this much would be to overlook the rationale for requiring that one expect enjoyment. The rationale lies in a certain link between enjoyment and justification. The first point to note is that the expectation of enjoyment is—other things being equal—a justification for acting so as to secure the enjoyment; indeed, I take it to be in part definitive of the concept of a justification of action that "Because I expect to enjoy it" is—other things being equal—a justification for the action in question.

It is worth seeing why the "other things being equal" rider is required. Consider this case. Smith sees a magazine on the seat next to him in the train station; he realizes that it contains pornographic photographs of children. Several months ago he picked up a similar magazine that he found in the train station; his intention was to throw it away without looking at it. Curiosity got the better of him, however, and he opened it to find, to his horror, that he enjoyed looking at the photos. Forewarned by this experience, Smith expects that he would enjoy the pictures in the magazine next to him. However, Smith is committed to realizing the self-concept *respecting human dignity*, and he takes this commitment to be incompatible with enjoying the pictures. Given the strength and centrality of this commitment, Smith would hate himself himself if—despite being forewarned—he opened the magazine and enjoyed the pictures. In light of the self-hatred that enjoying the pictures would induce, Smith—correctly, surely—takes the expectation of enjoyment not to be a justification for acting so as to secure the enjoyment, but a justification for acting so as not to secure it.

In a happy life, the relation between the expectation of enjoyment and justification is just the opposite. One finds in the expectation of enjoyment a justification for living as one does: one has the affirmative attitude that consists in the enjoyment-justified expectation that one will realize one's self-concepts sufficiently often. To see this, consider Mason before learning of his condition. He expected to realize his self-concepts sufficiently often and took this motivating expectation to be a justification for doing so, where part of his basis for taking the expectation to a justification was that the expected to enjoy realizing the self-concepts in question. Let us express the fact that Mason took the expectation to be a justification (at least in part) on this basis by saying that the expectation was *enjoyment-justified*. After learning of his condition, defiance replaces enjoyment as a source of justification. What I suggest is that in a happy life, one has the enjoyment-justified motivating expectation that one will realize sufficiently often the self-concepts to which one is committed. This enjoyment-justified motivating expectation is the affirmative attitude.

Adding the requirement of this affirmative attitude to the Sidgwickian condition yields the following. Let T be a maximal period of commitment to the collection of expansive self-concepts C. Then one is leading a happy life during T only if

(1) during T one enjoys the realization of the self-concepts in C sufficiently often,
(2) throughout T, one has the enjoyment-justified expectation that one will continue to realize the self-concepts in C sufficiently often.

Note that it is not necessary to require that the expectation be a motive since (as we argued above) it follows from the definition of commitment that it must be. It is also not necessary to state explicitly in (2) that one expects to enjoy realizing the self-concepts; it follows that one does from the fact that the expectation is enjoyment-justified.

Are these conditions sufficient? They may be. Whether they are depends on the solution to the problem raised in the Introduction about whether actually satisfying—as opposed to merely thinking one is satisfying—one's desires is required for leading a happy life. Consider the restaurant-owner example again. The owner is committed to realizing various self-concepts: *running a restaurant, enjoying the love of his wife and children, employing an astute business sense,* and so on. He does not realize any of these self-concepts: the manager really runs the restaurant, the owner has no business sense, his wife and children are at best indifferent to him, and so on. But this is no barrier to his enjoying the realization of his self-concepts sufficiently often. To enjoy the realization of a self-concept, the owner need only believe that the relevant experience or activity realizes the self-concept. The owner does have such beliefs since he is deceived into thinking that he runs the restaurant, has an astute business sense, and is the object of his wife's and children's love. So the owner's life is filled with the enjoyment that is the central component of a happy life, and in the midst of his enjoyment, the owner would certainly describe himself as leading a happy life.

Would he be right? I do not think so. Suppose that the owner were challenged to show that the expectation provides a justification for action. A sufficiently thorough examination of his life would reveal that he has not realized, and cannot expect to realize, his self-concepts. In light of this fact, I suggest that he should not count as leading a happy life: the happy life does not contain, in the way just illustrated, the seeds of the destruction of the motive that one takes to provide a justification for living as one does.

The notion of commitment (again) is the key to seeing the idea. Commitment involves forming beliefs as to how to realize one's self-concepts sufficiently often. Now we try—more or less, at least— to have adequate grounds for our beliefs; a being that did not ever, in any way, try to have adequate for its beliefs would not really be a being that formed beliefs. One cannot count as a believer unless one tries—more or less—to have adequate grounds for one's beliefs. Beliefs as to how to realize self-concepts sufficiently often are no exception; however, in trying to have adequate grounds for these beliefs, the owner may well discover that his belief that he will realize his self-concepts sufficiently often is unwarranted. It is in this sense that the owner's way of life is potentially destructive of the very motive that he has for living as he does. It would not be potentially destructive of this motive if the owner actually were realizing his self-concepts sufficiently often.

I suspect that it is part of our concept of happiness that the happy person is safeguarded against this sort of potential destructiveness by virtue of actually realizing the self-concepts to which he is committed. In support of this point, suppose you wish Smith's newborn baby a happy life. It seems quite plausible to suggest that, among the eventualities incompatible with your wish, is the one in which the baby grows up to live a life like the restaurant owner's—a life in which, as a result of deception, he only thinks he is getting what he wants.[9] However, except for such examples, I do not see any further considerations to bring forward to establish this claim. So although I will write the requirement of actual realization into the final account of happiness, we should regard the requirement as having a somewhat provisional nature. In part, my reluctance to regard the condition as sufficient derives from worries about religious belief. Suppose that a mystic devotes herself to realizing the self-concept *union with The One* (and similar related self-concepts), and—let us suppose—the One does not exist. It follows that the mystic, like the restaurant owner, is not realizing the self-concepts to which she is committed, but does it follow that the mystic is not

9. The example is from Richard Kraut, "Two Conceptions of Happiness," *Philosophical Review*, 88, no. 2 (April 1979).

leading a happy life? I must admit to some inclination to answer yes; however, I must also admit to the opposite inclination: surely— I sometimes want to say—the mystical ecstasy of even merely apparent union with The One should be enough for happiness. Perhaps the solution is to treat such cases as exceptions to the general requirement of actual realization; there is a rationale for doing so. We located the rationale for the requirement of actual realization in the fact that we try to have adequate grounds for our beliefs— the point of the requirement being to safeguard the happy person from discovering, through rational self-examination, that he has no adequate ground for his belief that he has been realizing his self-concepts sufficiently often. Religious beliefs, however, tend to survive the demonstration that they lack adequate rational grounds, so perhaps we can, in the case of lives built around such beliefs, dispense with the requirement of actual realization.

With the foregoing qualifications and caveats, I suggest that the following conditions are necessary and sufficient for leading a happy life. Let T be a maximal period of commitment to the collection of expansive self-concepts C.

> One is leading a happy life during T if and only if
> (1) during T, one both realizes and enjoys the realization of the self-concepts in C sufficiently often,
> (2) throughout T, one has the enjoyment-justified expectation that one will continue to realize the self-concepts in C sufficiently often.

Two comments are in order. First, the expectation specified in the second condition is not bounded with respect to the future; one expects to continue—not to continue until next Tuesday or until one is forty but simply to continue into the future without any definite endpoint.[10] Second, this definition of leading a happy life is relativized to maximal periods of commitment because—given the role that commitment to self-concepts plays in leading a happy

---

10. This raises interesting questions about the expectation of death. Can one who expects to die at a specific time—perhaps tomorrow—count as leading a happy life? Or does an unhappy end await us all? The answer depends on exactly what self-concepts one is committed to at the time of one's death. Perhaps it is possible to be committed to self-concepts that allow one to think that even as one is dying, one will be realizing those self-concepts sufficiently often.

life—such periods have a certain primacy in determining whether one is leading a happy life. Such periods are the natural ones to look at in determining whether one is realizing one's self-concepts sufficiently often; one wants to know whether—overall, that is, throughout the maximal period of commitment—one has realized those self-concepts sufficiently often. We can count a person as leading a happy life for a part of a maximal period of commitment when he satisfies the definition when it is relativized to that partial time period. Now consider a period of time T^* that spans more than one maximal period of commitment. Thus:

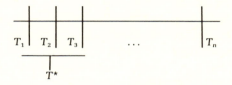

A sufficient condition of leading a happy life during T^* is that one should lead a happy life during all the component periods.

This is not a necessary condition, of course. One could have failed to lead a happy life during T_2, but this could be outweighed by the fact that one led a happy life during other components. One leads a happy life during T^* just in case the happy periods compensate sufficiently for the unhappy ones. I will not try to be any more precise than this; given our purposes here there is no need to be, and in any case, a precise answer may not be possible.

There are two objections to the definition that we should consider. First, suppose that you have a headache and S-desire to take an aspirin to be rid of it. Surely, the life in which you satisfy this desire is happier—by very little, perhaps, but still happier—than the life in which you do not satisfy the desire and suffer with the headache. The objection is that we cannot explain this fact, for on the above analysis, the only desires whose satisfaction is relevant to one's happiness are E-desires to realize self-concepts to which one is committed. This objection is based on a misunderstanding. To see this, consider that the analysis of leading a happy life is intended to draw the line between lives that are happy and lives that are not. Consider two lives that fall on the happy side of this line. The lives are exactly alike except that, in one, the person satisfies the S-desire to take aspirin so as to be rid of a headache;

in the other, this desire goes unsatisfied. Nothing in the analysis of happiness bars us from recognizing that the first life is (slightly) happier than the second. The definition is, after all, not a definition of what it is for one happy life to be happier than another happy life; it is an account of what is it for a life to be happy at all. It may well be that S-desires are important in determining when one happy life is happier than another.[11]

The second objection is to the expectation requirement. Suppose that all is going well with Kimberly; she is realizing and enjoying the realization of her self-concepts. However, at this moment, she is depressed and insists that everything is hopeless. All she can see before herself is failure. But the depression is brief, and when it passes, she is once more optimistic. Does she, in the midst of her depression, fail to expect that she will continue to enjoy the realization of her self-concepts sufficiently often? If so, her transient depression is enough to make her count as not leading a happy life. And this seems wrong. Transient depressions, black moods, and the like can occur during one's life even though one counts as leading a happy life throughout that period. The answer is that, in the midst of her depression, Kimberly still does count as expecting to continue to enjoy the realization of her self-concepts sufficiently often. A transient depression or a brief black mood is not enough to make one count as lacking the expectation. Indeed, these are just the sorts of cases in which, were Kimberly to express her dismal view of her future, we would insist, "That is not what you really think." The matter would be different if she were always depressed or always in a black mood, but then these are not cases of leading a happy life.

The Condition of Adequacy

The account of leading a happy life meets the condition of adequacy given in the Introduction. With one exception, the account entails the four conditions of the initial characterization of leading a happy life and answers the questions that this characterization left unanswered.

11. I am in this paragraph indebted to Gregory Vlastos, who attributes a similar position to Plato.

(1) One is leading a happy life only if one satisfies one's important desires sufficiently often.

The analysis entails this condition. As we noted in the Introduction, the important desires are desires that one must satisfy to count as leading a happy life. The account allows us to identify these desires in a noncircular way: they are the E-desires to realize self-concepts to which one is committed. What counts as realizing these desires sufficiently often is determined by one's commitment. To be committed to realizing a collection C of self-concepts sufficiently often is for there to be some (roughly and approximately specifiable) frequency of realization such that one is committed to realizing the concepts in C that frequently. If one realizes the self-concepts to which one is committed that frequently, one satisfies one's important desires sufficiently often.

(2) One is leading a happy life only if one believes that one is satisfying one's important desires sufficiently often.

In the Introduction, I suggested that the reason this was a necessary condition of happiness is that the happy person has a certain "affirmative attitude" toward his life. The account provides a characterization of this affirmative attitude: it is the enjoyment-justified expectation that one will realize sufficiently often the self-concepts to which one is committed.

(3) One is leading a happy life only if, in addition to satisfying one's important desires sufficiently often, one also enjoys satisfying those desires.

When we discussed condition 3, we noted that there were important and systematic connections among the concepts of happiness, enjoyment, and personhood, and we said that an adequate analysis of leading a happy life should characterize and explain these conditions. The definition I have given is built around explicit accounts of personhood and enjoyment, and it not only entails condition 3, it also provides an illuminating and informative characterization of the relations among happiness, enjoyment, and personhood.

(4) One is leading a happy life only if, in addition to satisfying one's important desires sufficiently often, what one
desires: (a) one takes to be worthy of desire and (b) really is
worthy of desire.

The account of happiness entails part (a)—at least on one inter-
pretation of 'taken to be worthy of desire'. Consider that the important desires are the E-desires to realize the self-concepts to which
one is committed; by virtue of this commitment, one can be described as valuing the realization of those self-concepts. Recall the
connection between commitment and valuing: to be committed to
realizing self-concepts is to value their realization, in the sense that
to value A is to have a standing commitment to selecting A over
(at least some) other alternatives. We argued earlier that one is
leading a happy life only if one enjoys what one values, so it follows
that, with respect to important desires, one who is leading a happy
life values what one desires. In this sense, one who is leading a
happy life takes what one desires to be worthy of desire: one values
it.

What about part (b)? We can put the question this way: to lead
a happy life, must what one values really be of value? The question
is obscure to the extent that it is obscure what it means that something really is of value. I will address this question briefly in the
Afterword, where I will suggest that we explain being of value in
terms of the justification of action. Here I will simply point out
that, even without an explanation of what it is to be of value, there
are examples that suggest that the account does not entail (b). In
the Introduction, we considered a person—the Counter—who devotes as much time as possible to laying out geometric patterns
with string and counting the blades of grass within, keeping a record
of the location, date, pattern, and number. The Counter is committed to realizing the self-concept *being a grass counter* and various related concepts, and he certainly may, in realizing these self-
concepts, satisfy the conditions of the definition of happiness. But
surely if the realization of any collection of self-concepts is to count
as not really of value, the realization of The Counter's self-concepts
surely lacks value.

It is a virtue, not a defect, of the account that it does not entail
(b). Even if we think that there is such a thing as being of value,

we must recognize that lives spent in the realization of self-concepts that in fact lack value can be happy ones. Misspent lives need not be unhappy ones. As we will see in the Afterword, this does not mean that misspent but happy lives are beyond criticism—even criticism that the person himself is committed to accepting. "You are not really happy" is not the only such criticism.

This completes the discussion of happiness; let us turn briefly, and speculatively, to the topic of justification.

Afterword

In the Introduction, I suggested using the accounts of freedom, personhood, and happiness as a guide to the content of the notion of a justification of an action. The idea was that by seeing what the notion does, we could see what it is. Although this brief Afterword is not the place to pursue this strategy, there are two points that merit some discussion.

Happiness as the Ultimate Source of Justification

A long tradition regards happiness as the ultimate source of the justification of action. Aristotle is a good example. Consider his remarks on the notion of "the good." He says that the good

> is evidently something different in different actions and in each art: it is one thing in medicine, another in strategy, and another again in each of the other arts. What then is the good of each? It is not that for the sake of which everything else is done? That means that it is health in the case of medicine, victory in the case of strategy, a house in the case of building, a different thing in the case of different arts, and in all actions and choices it is the end. For it is for the sake of the end that all else is done. Thus, if there is some one end for all that we do, this would be the good attainable by action; if there are several ends, they will be the goods obtainable by action.[1]

1. *Nicomachean Ethics*, trans. Martin Ostwald (Indianapolis: Bobbs-Merrill, 1962), 1097a16–24.

Aristotle of course thinks that "there is some one end for all that we do": happiness. Happiness is "that for the sake of which everything else is done." Now, "that for the sake of which everything else is done" is what serves as the justification for doing "everything else." So happiness is the ultimate source of all justification.

Although this view may be defensible given Aristotle's account of happiness as an activity of the soul in conformity with virtue, it is not defensible given the definition of happiness developed in the last chapter. Let us consider the view in this form:

> (*) A desire to φ provides a justification for φing if and only if φing is conducive to one's leading a happy life.

There are examples that strongly suggest that (*) is false, for there are examples that suggest that commitment to self-concepts is— independently of considerations about happiness—a source of justification.

Suppose that you are committed to realizing a collection of self-concepts C that includes the self-concepts *political activist, having the courage of one's convictions, challenging authority*, and *having a clear sense of justice*. If you act so as to realize these self-concepts, you will—as you realize—not lead a happy life. The government will imprison you and persecute your family. Nonetheless, you persist in your commitment to C: you form beliefs as to how to realize these self-concepts sufficiently often, and you act in accord with these beliefs; you take the motives provided by these beliefs to be justifications for realizing the self-concepts, even though you are fully aware that in acting in accord with these beliefs you are condemning yourself to unhappiness.

It follows from (*) that you do not have a justification for acting as you do. But how can this be right? Suppose you are asked why you do not change your commitment to self-concepts since it condemns you to unhappiness. You answer that commitment to the self-concepts in C is what makes you the person that you are. To ask you to change this commitment as radically as you would have to do to avoid imprisonment is to ask you to make a fundamental change: it is to ask you to be a different kind of person. The strength of your commitment to C is such that you refuse. It is not that you do not want to be happy; you do want happiness, but you want it through realizing the self-concepts in C. If the price of happiness is abandoning your commitment, you judge the price to be too high. Surely, it is implausible to deny that you could be right, to deny that you have a justification for meeting your commitment to the self-concepts in C. On the contrary, we should recognize commitment as a source of justification, which is (at least to some extent) independent of considerations about happiness.

The relation between happiness and justification is far more complicated than anything like (*). Any adequate analysis must provide a place for the possible opposition between justificatory considerations deriving from one's commitment to self-concepts and considerations about what would make one happy.

There is an additional problem with (*) that also promises to be a problem with any revision of (*). (*) suffers from a kind of circularity, for in defining happiness we appeal to the notion of justification. To lead a happy life, one must enjoy realizing self-concepts to which one is committed. Now, one is committed to realizing a self-concept only if one takes the desire to realize that self-concept to provide a justification for action. So if (*) is true, what is the content of my thought, "This desire provides a justification"? Specifying what justification is introduces the concept of happiness; saying what happiness is reintroduces the concept of justification.

Justification and Value

I would like to comment very briefly and speculatively on the relation between justification and value. Suppose that we follow Aristotle is identifying that which makes an experience or activity of value—what Aristotle calls "the good" of the experience or activity—with that for the sake of which the experience is sought or the activity performed. As we noted earlier, "that for the sake of which everything else is done" is whatever serves as the justification for doing "everything else." We are explaining what it is to be of value in terms of justification, so an analysis of justification would yield an analysis of what it is to be of value.

My hope is that such an account would provide a basis for criticizing The Counter—in terms The Counter would be committed to accepting. For The Counter, by virtue of being a person, takes desires to provide justifications for action. Thus he has and employs a certain notion of justification. It could be that, in light of this notion of justification, The Counter's way of life lacks value, that he really has no—or no adequate—justification for realizing the self-concepts to which he is committed.

One might hope for more along these lines that just a criticism of The Counter's life. One might hope that the concept of the justification of action—the concept that every person has and employs—has the following property: a person never has a justification, or never an adequate one, for immoral action while always having a decisive justification for moral action.

Index